Sew the ....

Contemporary Wardrobe

For 18-Inch Dolls

JOAN HINDS

Published by

krause publications

700 East State Street • Iola, WI 54990-0001
715/445-2214 • FAX: 715/445-4087   www.krause.com

Please call or write for our free catalog of publications. Our toll-free number to place an order or obtain a free catalog is 800-258-0929 or please use our regular business telephone, 715-445-2214.

Library of Congress Catalog Number: 2001097822

ISBN: 0-87349-375-3

Printed in the United States of America

Photos by Jeff Frey & Associates Photography, Inc.
Illustrations by Kathy Marsaa

The following registered trademark terms and companies appear in this publication:
American Girl® by Pleasant Company, Collector's Lane®, Creative Doll Company®, Götz® Company, Lycra®, Springfield Collection®, Velcro®.

DEDICATION

To all the sewing teachers everywhere – whether they are mothers, other family members, or formally recognized teachers – who continue to promote their love of textiles and fiber arts.

ACKNOWLEDGMENTS

I wish to offer sincere appreciation to these people, who assisted and supported me with this book. An enormous thank you goes to:

A new friend, Marilee Sagat, a millinery expert extraordinaire, for her design assistance with the hats and accessories, and her help with "t-shirt construction."

My friend and skilled pattern tester, Lauri Cushing.

The fabulous photographers, Tigg and Rolf, at Jeff Frey and Associates.

Kathy Marsaa, my illustrator, who has the uncanny ability to read my mind.

My husband Fletcher, son Kevin, and daughter Rebecca for their never-ending help with proofreading, fabric color choice, doll hair-styling, and computer skills.

The readers of my newsletter, *Fancywork's Best News,* for their enthusiasm and our shared love of doll costuming.

The wonderfully enthusiastic staff of Krause Publications, including Barbara Case, my editor, and Brenda, Don, and Julie.

Dianne Giancola, with Prym-Dritz Corp., for her willingness to help promote sewing for dolls.

And most importantly, many thanks to my "focus group," including Siri, Bethany, Katie, Gwen, Marta, and mothers Jan and Char.

TABLE OF CONTENTS

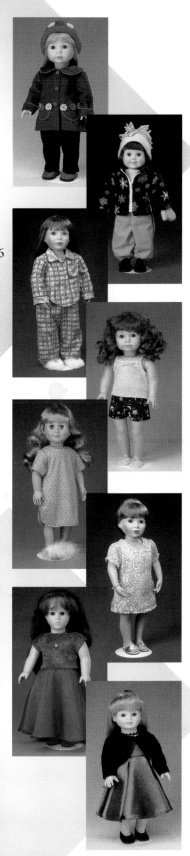

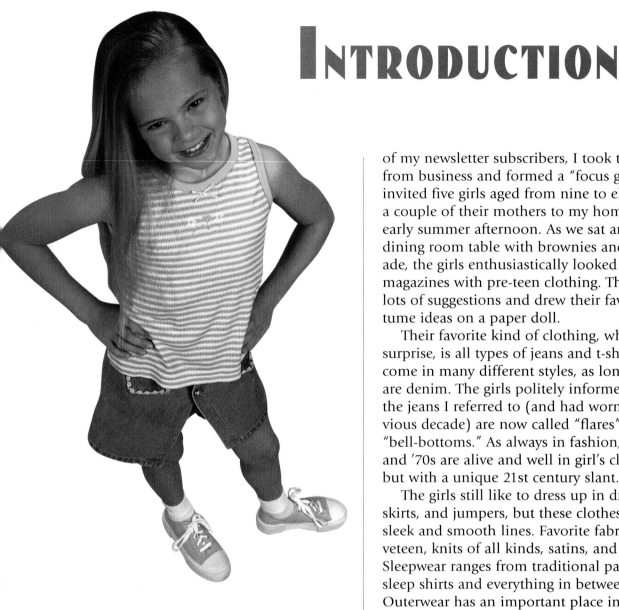

INTRODUCTION

of my newsletter subscribers, I took the lead from business and formed a "focus group." I invited five girls aged from nine to eleven and a couple of their mothers to my home on an early summer afternoon. As we sat around my dining room table with brownies and lemonade, the girls enthusiastically looked at many magazines with pre-teen clothing. They had lots of suggestions and drew their favorite costume ideas on a paper doll.

Their favorite kind of clothing, which is no surprise, is all types of jeans and t-shirts. Jeans come in many different styles, as long as they are denim. The girls politely informed me that the jeans I referred to (and had worn in a previous decade) are now called "flares" and not "bell-bottoms." As always in fashion, the '60s and '70s are alive and well in girl's clothing, but with a unique 21st century slant.

The girls still like to dress up in dresses, skirts, and jumpers, but these clothes have sleek and smooth lines. Favorite fabrics are velveteen, knits of all kinds, satins, and sheers. Sleepwear ranges from traditional pajamas to sleep shirts and everything in between. Outerwear has an important place in their wardrobe, especially up here in the northland. Coats are short and swingy, reminiscent again of past decades. Jackets are made from fleece fabric, a new staple in the sewing market.

The girls loved all the accessories that are designed to accent today's clothing, such as hats, purses, and jewelry. In fact, for my focus group two girls showed up wearing the same hat!

Now that I was armed with dozens and dozens of suggestions, I had the difficult but wonderful task of choosing the outfits and accessories. The logical solution was to categorize the clothing as a department store does. They all have departments for "separates,"

What Girls Want

$\mathcal{I}$ have designed many, many doll costumes in a variety of books for the ever-popular 18-inch doll in the last ten years. These have ranged from fantasy and fairy tale gowns to simple play wear. One theme I have heard over and over is, "My daughter/granddaughter wants to dress her doll in clothing that resembles what girls wear today!" Thus the idea for contemporary clothing for 18-inch dolls was born.

The next step was to find out what types of clothing young girls like and how they want to dress their dolls. With a suggestion from one "special occasions," "outerwear," "sleepwear," and of course, "accessories!" The photos for the book, however, must have a doll in a complete outfit, so I have combined pants with shirts and tops with skirts. You may choose to put the hooded sweatshirt with the long denim skirt, or the flared jeans, or the cargo pants… the combinations are endless!

Don't limit yourself to these sixteen outfits. You can create many, many outfits with the patterns for the clothing items included here.

What Dolls Will These Patterns Fit?

The American Girl doll by the Pleasant Company took the doll market by storm in the 1980s. This rebirth of childlike play dolls spawned other manufacturers to create their own brand of 18-inch vinyl child dolls. The faces are all unique, but the cloth bodies are sufficiently similar to exchange clothing, particularly dresses. Arms, legs, hands, and feet sometimes vary enough to require different sleeve lengths and different shoe sizes, but most of them can wear the clothing in this book.

Even within a single brand, stuffed cloth bodies may vary from doll to doll. The bodies don't come from a mold and there is a human element involved in their fullness. Also, dolls that remain in stands or are actively played with may become slimmer over time. In most cases, the most critical measurement is the waist. The patterns in this book presume an 11½ inch waist. This measurement is most important when making garments with a waistband. For this reason, whenever possible,

all of the pants and skirts have elastic at least in the back waistband to allow for different waist sizes.

The dolls pictured in this book are from a variety of manufacturers. In the case of the Collector's Lane and the Springfield Collection, be sure to make note that the arms and ankle measurements are slightly narrower than the American Girl doll, so adjust the wrist and ankle measurements in the appropriate garments. The Creative Doll Company doll has slightly wider hips and needs more depth in the crotch area, so a trial made from muslin will help in fitting pants.

If you are stuffing your own Springfield Collection doll, be sure to follow the instructions on the package for the correct amount of fiberfill needed. Begin stuffing the arms and the tops of the legs first and work toward the waist. As you are stuffing the chest area, keep the post that extends down from the head in the center of the body so that the head will remain straight up and down.

As long as this type of doll remains popular, more brands will appear each year. Be aware that they may need slight adjustments in waistbands, hem and sleeve lengths, etc. Try things on your doll as you construct the garments to make sure of the fit and accommodate variances.

Before You Begin…

After you have chosen your first project, you will be anxious to start sewing right away. A few words are necessary before you start your doll's new contemporary wardrobe. Please read this section carefully for general sewing instructions.

Measurements of your doll are an absolute must. Start a chart of all the pertinent measurements you might need. These would be: waist, upper arm, wrist, neck, and ankle circumference, back shoulder width, and back neck-to-crotch length. A new narrow tape measure is available to help you with this task. It is narrow enough to wrap around the smallest of doll parts.

Next, you should gather your equipment. Begin with a sewing machine, sewing shears, pins, seam gauge, and washout marker. A serger is not necessary, even for the knit garments, but it helps with construction and gives seam allowances a clean finish. A steam iron is a must. A "mini-iron" designed for the quilting industry is perfect for the small areas in doll clothing construction. Small ironing boards are essential for pressing small sleeves, collars, pant legs, etc.

Now you can decide which separates to make. Note that the outfits can be put together many different ways. Your doll lover may adore the flared jeans but want them to be worn with the short-sleeve t-shirt and the rolled brim crocheted hat. Perhaps she wants the capri pants made from satin and the crushed velvet top made from confetti sequin fabric for a dressy look. Use your imagination to mix and match the separates for an infinite number of outfits for all seasons and occasions.

The embroidery methods and trims used in these garments can be easily interchanged. I have used a couple of iron-on motifs and one motif stitched by an embroidery machine. Any garment can have either type of embellishment. I applied the trims to the capri pants and the flared jeans, but you may want trim on the cargo pants. Just measure the area to be trimmed and zigzag it in place.

Fabric selection has always been my favorite part of garment design. The fabric that shows up overwhelmingly in the wardrobe of the "girl of today" is denim, denim, and more denim! You will have more success if you choose a lighter weight denim fabric for doll clothes. The fabric stores carry a variety of colors, weights, and even a few prints. Denim combines well with knits that are ideal for the perennial t-shirt. Look for sheer overlays, crushed velvets, satins, and sequin fabrics for party clothes.

Please note that all seam allowances are $\frac{1}{4}$ inch unless specified otherwise. We have become accustomed to using a $\frac{5}{8}$ inch seam allowance for garment sewing, so the transition to narrower seams may take a little effort. Some of us tend to make the seams slightly wider than $\frac{1}{4}$ inch. This may affect the fit. An easy way to be sure you have accurate seam allowances is to use a quilting presser foot that has a width of $\frac{1}{4}$ inch built in. Be aware that the foot has a small hole so you cannot zigzag stitch without switching presser feet. Another option is to use an edge stitching foot. If your sewing machine can adjust the needle position from side-to-side, you can move the needle so that the stitching will be exactly $\frac{1}{4}$ inch from the fabric edge.

Most of the garments that close in the back have an overlap of approximately $\frac{1}{2}$ inch. While it is always safer to have the particular doll you are sewing for in front of you, if you are sewing for a doll not in your possession, this is a measurement to note.

T-shirts are made from knit fabrics with a horizontal stretch. Some sewers have had trouble fitting the shirts over the doll's head if the fabric or ribbing does not adequately stretch. The t-shirts in this book are designed to have a center back seam that opens at the top with a Velcro strip for closure. This was done so that the shirts will fit over the doll's head, no matter how much stretch the knit has. The only shirt that doesn't is the cap-sleeve t-shirt. The t-shirt front and back pattern pieces have the same width, so they can be interchanged with all the sleeves (the length may be different, however). You then can make any of the t-shirts with or without the back opening.

Seam finishes are only mentioned when absolutely necessary. Feel free to finish the seam allowances, as you prefer, either with a serger or zigzag stitching. Some machines have a three-step zigzag, which allows the fabric to be stitched without rolling or bunching.

You have measured your doll, found the appropriate pattern pieces, picked out fabrics and trims. Now... let's begin!!

Helping Children Learn to Sew

All of us have fond memories of our first experiences with sewing or needlework. Usually this occurred at the knee of an older relative, such as a grandmother, mother, or aunt. Many of us learned to sew while quite young, and a favorite project was doll clothes. But sometimes it can be under the tutelage of a home economics teacher, or 4-H or Girl Scout leader.

I will always be indebted to my first home economics teacher. She allowed me to make a matching vest to go with my skirt (which covered *advanced* techniques such as facings). She told the class that my outfit was right out of the fashion district in *New York*!

This experience could still happen today. While home economics with a sewing curriculum may not often be taught in schools, we can each be a mentor to an enthusiastic child. The favorite projects that excited young beginners in the past are still the same – doll clothing! Children are much more eager to learn when the lessons apply to a project that they desire. Dressing a beloved doll fits the bill.

If you are lucky enough to have a child to teach sewing skills, this book will help you get started. The first step is to choose the projects that are suitable for beginners. Children can construct most of the clothing patterns, but some garments may need more assistance than others. I provide suggestions with each garment to help you decide if it appropriate for your student.

Everyone likes to pick out their favorite fabrics in their favorite colors. Let your student accompany you to the fabric store. Remember, picking out fabric for one or two outfits will not be as overwhelming as choosing fabric for many outfits.

All children can be taught to find patterns on the tissue paper pullout and to cut them out. They can be shown how to lay them out on the fabric with the correct grain and how to pin them to the fabric. The pieces are small enough that they will be able to pin them without difficulty. Be sure your student is capable of handling sewing shears without the danger of injury.

Next, set up a sewing area for the lesson. Your sewing space will most likely be perfect, but some children have legs too short to reach the foot pedal. If this is the case, try placing the pedal on a sturdy box. Another idea is to mount the foot pedal to the wall of the desk or filing cabinet nearby and use it as a knee pedal. If your child is quite young, you may want to have them sit on your lap and help you guide the fabric in the sewing machine while you work the foot control. Be sure that all the equipment they need is handy (pins, seam gauge, iron and board, etc.).

Garments that have straight seams are best to begin with. These include the capri pants, pull-on pants, jumpers, and skirts. Your student may only be able to do part of the garment construction at first and need your assistance often. After trying a few garments they will need less help. For curved seams, you may want to draw the seam line onto the wrong side of the fabric with a washout marker to help them. Be sure that they know how to secure the seam at the start and end. Whether your machine has a button that automatically "fixes" the seam, or you need to take a few stitches in reverse, the seam will tend not to unravel. This will eliminate a lot of unnecessary frustration. Also, young sewers can use zigzag stitches to finish seams. It is best to leave the narrow straps, bias bindings, and zipper insertion for those who are more experienced.

Beginning students can also use sergers. They can sew the shoulder and side seams together in the t-shirts. The sleeves and neck bindings need to be eased into place, so only children with sewing experience should try them.

For all of us, the embellishment is often the most fun part of garment construction! Children love to use the decorative stitches and the embroidery component on sewing machines. (My son was interested in sewing in grade school, but only wanted to use the decorative stitches.) Let them pick out their favorite designs to be embroidered on jumpers, t-shirts, and pants. They will need assistance in setting up the embroidery unit on the machine and with hooping the fabric. They can choose their favorite decorative stitches to be placed on all types of garments. A favorite embellishment is stitching their name or their doll's name on something they have made themselves.

Don't forget the accessories! Not all of the accessories in this book require sewing and they are good projects to give beginners confidence and a sense of accomplishment. The crystal beaded necklace and bracelet can be done by the smallest of children, since no needle is used. Small fingers are sometimes better at beadwork than larger ones. The crocheted purse is a great project to learn to crochet. It is small enough to work up fast, keeping the child's interest.

Loving and concerned mentors can continue the sewing and crafting tradition into future generations. All it takes is one mentor and one child to begin.

Casual
Separates

Jean Jacket and A-Line Skirt

*T*he jean jacket has been a wardrobe staple since cowboys first wore them. Bikers wore them in the '50s, but now jean jackets show up in closets of people of all ages and from all lifestyles. A jean jacket typically has pockets in the front and a band around the bottom that fits above the hips. Today, they can have either decorative snap or button closures. I have finished mine with buttons and snaps underneath. You may wish to have actual buttonholes and buttons, or decorative snaps on yours. The details on this jacket, such as the topstitching and tiny pocket flaps make it a project for more experienced sewers.

The A-line skirt is also a wardrobe favorite. Bias-cut plaids are often seen in skirts for girls. This style works well for dolls, too. The skirt back is cut larger to allow for elastic in the back waistband. This will accommodate many waist measurements and insure proper fit. This skirt is an excellent one for beginning sewers. Small children may need help with the elastic casing.

The doll shown is a "Dress Me Götz" doll.

Jean Jacket

Pattern pieces #1, #2, #3, #4, #5, #6, #7, #8, #9, #10

Supplies:

¼ yd. dark blue light-
   weight denim fabric
7 buttons (³⁄₈″)
7 snaps
Gold topstitching thread
2.0 mm double needle

Jean Jacket

Instructions:

1. Cut two front yokes, two lower jacket fronts, one back yoke, one lower jacket back, four pocket flaps, two facings, one collar, two sleeves, two sleeve cuffs, and one jacket band from fabric.

2. With right sides together, sew two pocket flaps along the sides and pointed bottom edge. Leave the top edge open.

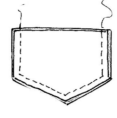

Clip the points, turn to the right side, and press. Using a double needle, topstitch with gold thread along all the sides a scant ⅛" from the sewn edges. Repeat with the other pocket.

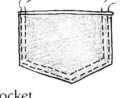

3. Using a double needle and gold thread, topstitch both lines on the lower jacket fronts as marked on the pattern piece. Place the top edge of one pocket on one of the top edges of the lower jacket front 1" from the center front. The topstitching on the jacket front will be underneath the pocket. Baste. Repeat with the other pocket.

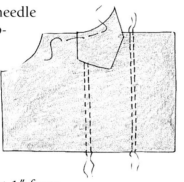

4. With right sides together, stitch the yoke fronts to the lower jacket fronts. Stitch the back yoke to the lower back jacket with right sides together.

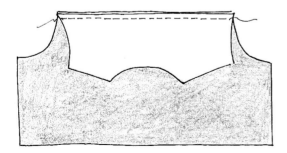

Press the seam allowances toward the yokes. With a double needle and gold thread, top-stitch on the yokes a scant ⅛" from each seam.

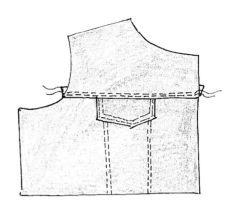

5. With right sides together, sew the fronts to the back at the shoulder seams.

6. Fold the collar in half lengthwise with right sides together. Stitch the short ends together. Turn to the right side and press. Topstitch with a double needle and gold thread a scant ⅛" from both ends and along the fold line.

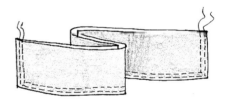

Place the center of the collar at the center of the neck edge of the back yoke and pin the collar to the neckline. Note that the collar does not reach all the way around to the center front. Baste.

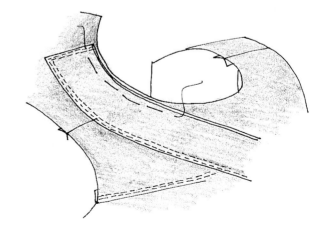

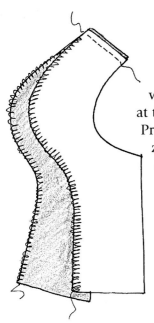

7. Stitch the facings with right sides together at the center back seam. Press open. Serge or zigzag the curved edge of the facing to finish the edge.

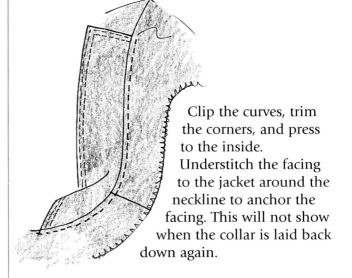

Clip the curves, trim the corners, and press to the inside. Understitch the facing to the jacket around the neckline to anchor the facing. This will not show when the collar is laid back down again.

8. Fold the sleeve cuffs in half lengthwise with the wrong sides together. Press. Stitch the cut edges to the bottom of the sleeves with right sides together.

Stitch the facing to the jacket along the center fronts and around the neckline.

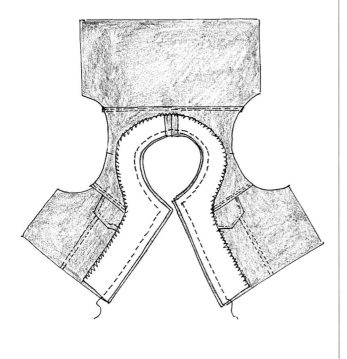

Press the seam allowances toward the sleeve. Using a single needle and gold thread, topstitch on both sides of the cuffs a scant ⅛" from the fold and seam.

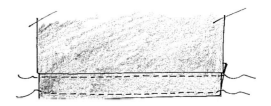

9. Gather the sleeve caps slightly. With right sides together, pin the sleeve caps to the armholes, easing as necessary. Stitch. Press the seam allowance towards the jacket. Topstitch along the jacket a scant ⅛" from the sleeve/jacket seam using a double needle and gold thread.

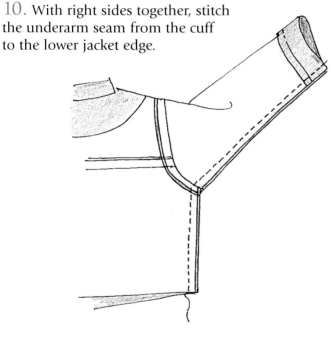

10. With right sides together, stitch the underarm seam from the cuff to the lower jacket edge.

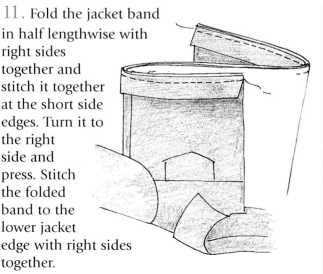

11. Fold the jacket band in half lengthwise with right sides together and stitch it together at the short side edges. Turn it to the right side and press. Stitch the folded band to the lower jacket edge with right sides together.

Press the seam towards the jacket. Using a single needle and gold thread, topstitch along the band a scant ⅛" from the folded edge, the center front edges, and the band/jacket seam.

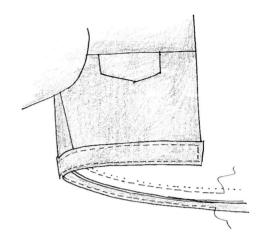

12. Sew five evenly spaced buttons to the right side of the jacket front. The last one should be placed over the jacket band. Sew one snap half under each button and the other snap half to the other side of the jacket. Sew a button to the center of each pocket flap.

Topstitching detail on the jean jacket front.

A-Line Skirt

Pattern pieces
#11, #12, #13

Supplies:

¼ yd. medium weight plaid fabric
4¾" elastic (¼" wide)

Instructions:

1. Cut one front skirt, one back skirt, and one waistband, all on the bias.

2. With right sides together, sew the side seams of the skirt.

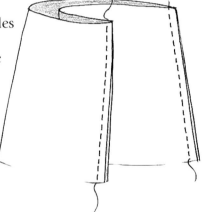

3. Stitch the short ends of the waistband with right sides together. Press the seam open. With the right side of the waistband facing the wrong side of the skirt, pin one edge of the waistband to the top edge of the skirt, placing the waistband seam at one side seam. Stitch.

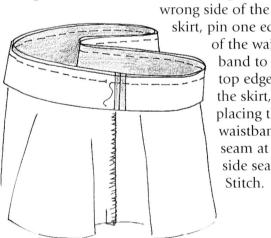

Press the remaining edge ¼" to the wrong side. Fold over the skirt and topstitch close to the folded edge, leaving approximately a 1" opening at each side seam to insert the elastic. Thread the elastic through the back waist casing and secure it to the waistband at each side seam. Sew the openings closed.

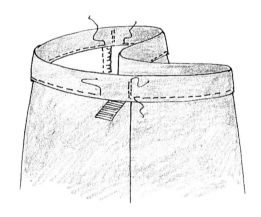

4. Zigzag or serge the bottom edge of the skirt. Press it ¼" to the wrong side and topstitch.

Khaki Cargo Pants, Long-Sleeve T-Shirt, and Fleece Vest

Many versions of khaki pants have been known in the fashion world under different names. In the middle of the 20th century they were known as "chinos." In the 1960s I remember wearing light-colored jeans known as "wheat jeans." Now they are simply called khakis. The pants I designed have a fly front and curved front pockets. The pants have optional "cargo" pockets on the sides. The pockets and fly may be challenging for children and will require some assistance.

T-shirts are a perennial wardrobe favorite for young and old alike. This version has long sleeves and a placket with a Velcro closure in the back for ease in dressing the doll. Children can sew the t-shirt with assistance in easing the sleeve caps and neckline ribbing.

Fleece garments are all the rage with young girls. This vest has a zipper front and Lycra binding to finish the armholes and lower edge. Most fabric stores have pre-cut strips, so you can purchase the amount you need and trim to the desired width. The zipper may pose a challenge to young sewers, but they should be able to sew the bindings with minimal assistance.

Khaki Cargo Pants

Pattern pieces
#14, #15, #16, #17, #18, #19

Supplies:
⅓ yd. khaki twill fabric
5½" elastic (¼" wide)
1 decorative snap

The doll shown is by the Götz Company.

Khaki Cargo Pants

Instructions:

1. Cut two fronts, two backs, two front pockets, two side pockets, two side pocket flaps, and one waistband.

2. With right sides together, put the curved edge of the pocket on one of the pants fronts and sew the seam along the cutout curve.

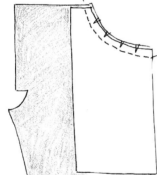

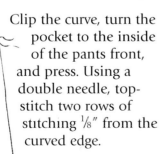

Clip the curve, turn the pocket to the inside of the pants front, and press. Using a double needle, top-stitch two rows of stitching ⅛" from the curved edge.

3. Fold up the pocket so it is even with the top edge of the pants front. Stitch the inside edges of the pocket together and finish the edges with zigzag stitching. Baste the side seam of the pants to the remaining side of the pocket. Repeat Steps 2 and 3 with the remaining pocket on the other side of the pants front.

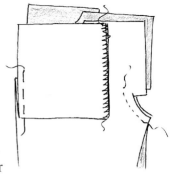

4. With right sides together, sew the fronts at the center seam only up to the dot marked on the pattern piece. Press the right fly edge ⅛" toward the wrong side and stitch.

5. Press the left fly toward the wrong side of the pants along the center front seam line. Stitch along the stitching line as marked on the pattern piece. Stitch the reinforcements on the fly as marked on the pattern piece.

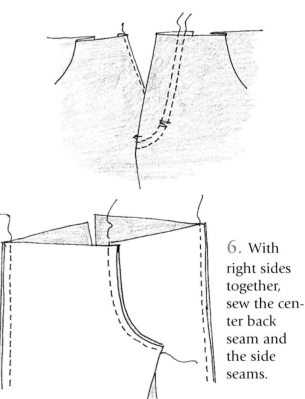

6. With right sides together, sew the center back seam and the side seams.

7. Make a box pleat in the center of the side pocket. Mark the center of the pocket at the top and bottom edge. Measure ¼" from the left

side at both the top and bottom and fold so they meet the center markings. Pin in place. Measure and mark ¼″ from the right side, fold to the center, and pin. Baste each pleat at the top and bottom edges and press.

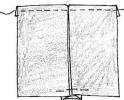

Press the top edge of the pocket ¼″ to the wrong side and stitch.

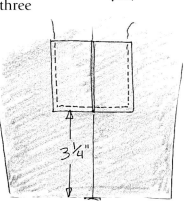

Press the remaining three sides of the pocket ¼″ to the wrong side. Center the pocket over the side seam of the pants 3¼″ from the hem edge and pin. Stitch the sides and bottom of the pocket ⅛″ from the pressed edges. Repeat with the remaining pocket.

3¼″

8. Fold the side pocket flap in half widthwise with right sides together. Stitch the sides, turn to the right side, and press.

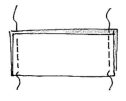

Topstitch along the sides and folded edge of the pocket ¼″ from the edge. Press the unstitched edges ¼″ to the wrong side.

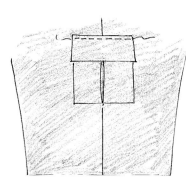

Pin the flap ¼″ above the pocket and stitch along the top edge.

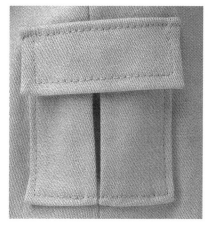

The side seam pocket on the khaki cargo pants.

9. Serge or zigzag stitch along one long edge of the waistband. With right sides together, and with the ends extending ¼″ beyond the center fronts of the pants, sew the long unfinished edge of the waistband to the pants.

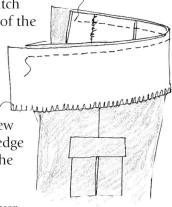

Fold the waistband over into the inside of the garment so the waistband is ½″ wide, tucking in the short ends. Topstitch in place, leaving a 1″ opening at each side seam for the casing. Thread the elastic through the back waistband and secure it at each side seam. Sew the openings closed.

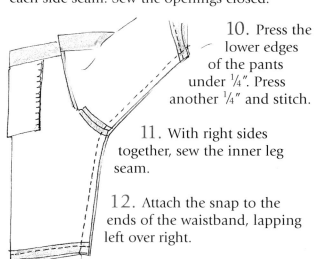

10. Press the lower edges of the pants under ¼″. Press another ¼″ and stitch.

11. With right sides together, sew the inner leg seam.

12. Attach the snap to the ends of the waistband, lapping left over right.

Long-Sleeve T-Shirt

Pattern pieces #20, #21, #22

Supplies:

¼ yd. knit fabric

8″ x 1½″ piece of ribbing

2″ Velcro strip

Instructions:

1. Cut one front, two backs, and two sleeves from knit fabric.

2. Using a narrow zigzag stitch, sew the center back seam to the dot marked on the pattern piece. Serge or zigzag each side of the back seam allowance separately, including the unstitched part of the seam. Press the seam allowances open and topstitch the open area of the seam.

3. With right sides together, sew the shoulder seams with a serger or zigzag stitch.

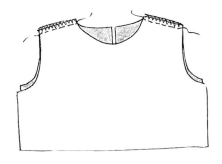

Fold the ribbing in half lengthwise with wrong sides together. Stitch the short ends and turn to the right side. Stretching the ribbing to fit the neck, serge or zigzag it to the neck opening.

4. Serge or zigzag stitch the lower edges of the sleeves. Press ¼″ to the wrong side and topstitch. With right sides together, serge or zigzag stitch the sleeves to the shirt armholes.

Serge or zigzag the underarm seam, starting at the sleeve hem and finishing at the lower edge of the shirt.

5. Serge or zigzag stitch the lower edge of the shirt and press ¼″ to the wrong side. Topstitch with a narrow zigzag stitch.

6. Sew Velcro to the back opening, lapping right over left.

Fleece Vest

Pattern pieces #23, #24, #25

Supplies:

¼ yd. fleece fabric
1 yd. Lycra fabric strip (1⅛″ wide)
6″ separating zipper

Instructions:

1. Cut two fronts, one back, and one collar from fabric.

2. With right sides together, stitch the fronts to the back at the shoulders.

3. Sew the one long edge of the collar to the neck edge of the vest with right sides together.

Pin one side of the center front edge of the vest (including the collar) ½″ to the wrong side. Place the bottom of one half of the zipper under the folded edge ½″ up from the lower edge of the vest. Pin the zipper to the folded and pinned edge so that the teeth are visible. (The zipper will extend up approx-

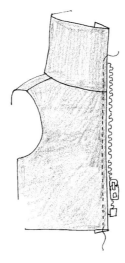

imately half of the collar width. If the zipper fabric extends beyond half the width of the collar, trim off the excess.) Stitch ¼″ from the folded edge. Repeat with the other side.

4. Fold the collar in half widthwise. Turn the long edge and both short ends ¼″ to the wrong side and pin, tucking in the collar seam line. Stitch ¼″ from the folded edges.

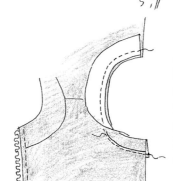

5. With right sides together, pin one edge of the Lycra strip on the seam line of an armhole. Stitch along the seam line and cut off the extra.

Fold the Lycra strip to the wrong side of the armhole and pin. Stitch over the previous seam on the right side, making sure to catch the Lycra strip underneath. Trim the Lycra strip close to the stitching on the wrong side. Repeat with the other armhole.

6. With right sides together, sew the side seams.

7. Pin the remaining Lycra strip to the right side of the vest ¼″ above the lower edge, stretching the Lycra strip slightly. Make sure the ends of the strip extend ¼″ beyond the center front seam and stitch. Fold the Lycra strip to the wrong side and pin, tucking in the short ends. Stitch over the previous seam on the right side, making sure to catch the Lycra strip underneath.

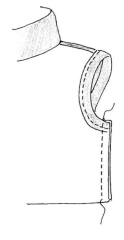

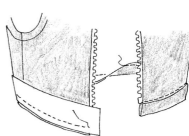

Denim Jumper and Short-Sleeve T-Shirt

*D*enim jumpers are very popular, especially those with straps and buckles like overalls. Jumpers can be embellished many different ways. One fun method is to embroider the front bib with your favorite designs. This jumper has a machine-embroidered design, but you can embroider by hand or purchase an embroidered appliqué. The hemline has braided trim at the bottom with decorative machine stitches above it. I chose to incorporate bobbin work, which is a heavy decorative thread that cannot fit through the eye of the needle, but is placed in the bobbin. It is not placed in the bobbin tension so that the thread will curl on the fabric. Since the threads are thick, the design is more prominent. Children love to use decorative stitches, and this jumper makes them easy to use.

The most common t-shirt is the short-sleeve version. This shirt can also have embroidery worked on the front or around the neckline just below the seam. This t-shirt provides a perfect opportunity for children to learn simple embroidery stitches, such as a circle of lazy daisies to make a flower.

Supplies:

$\frac{1}{3}$ yd. lightweight denim
$\frac{1}{4}$ yd. poly/cotton fabric for lining
2 mini overall buckles and slides
2 buttons ($\frac{3}{8}$")
$\frac{2}{3}$ yd. trim ($\frac{5}{8}$" wide)
2 spools of heavyweight rayon decorative thread
   in different colors
1 spool 40-weight machine embroidery thread
Tear-away stabilizer
Machine embroidery design on a disc or
   embroidered appliqué

The doll shown is by the Götz Company.

Denim Jumper
Pattern pieces #26, #27, #28, #29

Denim Jumper

Instructions:

1. Cut a piece of denim and stabilizer to fit the machine embroidery hoop. Stitch the embroidery design of your choice (make sure it will fit on the front bib pattern piece) with machine embroidery thread according to your machine's instructions. Remove it from the hoop and tear off the stabilizer. Center the front bib pattern piece over the design and cut out.

2. Cut one back bib, two straps, and two skirts from denim. Cut one front bib and one back bib from the lining fabric.

3. Press the long edges and the straight short end of the straps $\frac{1}{4}$" to the wrong side. Stitch close to the pressed edge with the machine embroidery thread. Put the slide and buckle on each strap end according to the package directions. The buckle can be adjusted for the correct length after the jumper is completed.

4. With right sides together, place the unstitched edges of the straps along the seam line of the back bib. The straps should touch in the middle and be $\frac{1}{4}$" from the side edges of the bib. Baste.

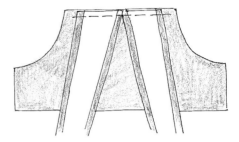

5. With right sides together, sew the lining to the front and back bib along the curved side edges and the top straight edge.

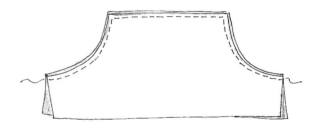

Clip the curves, trim the corners, and turn to the right side. Press. Stitch close to the edges with the machine embroidery thread.

6. Pin the wrong side of each skirt to a piece of stabilizer. Draw a line on the stabilizer $\frac{1}{2}$" from the lower skirt edges. Fill a bobbin with the heavyweight rayon thread. Put matching color thread through the needle and place the bobbin in the machine without placing the thread in the tension. Place the skirt under the presser foot with the stabilizer side up. Stitch a decorative stitch such as a row of diamonds on both the skirt front and back.

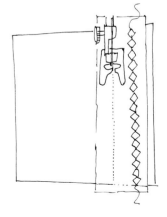

7. Draw another line ⅝″ above the first drawn line. Stitch another row of decorative stitches such as feather stitches as in Step 5, but with a different color heavyweight rayon thread, on both the front and back skirts.

8. Turn the skirt so the denim side is up. Put the 40-weight machine embroidery thread in the needle and regular sewing thread in the bobbin (in the tension). Center the presser foot between the two rows of embroidered stitches and stitch a row of decorative stitches such as hearts on both the front and back skirts. Tear away the stabilizer.

9. With right sides together, sew the front bib to the front skirt and the back bib to the back skirt. Press the seams toward the skirts. Stitch close to the seam line on the bibs with the machine embroidery thread.

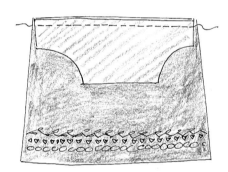

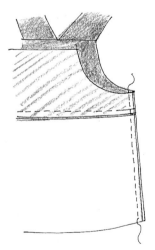

10. Sew the side seams with right sides together.

11. Serge or zigzag stitch the lower edge of the skirt. Place the braid below the embroidery rows and zigzag stitch the heading of the braid to the skirt, turning the end of the braid to the wrong side when you reach the start of the stitched braid.

12. Sew the buttons to the top corners of the front bib and adjust the straps if necessary.

Decorative stitching on the denim jumper skirt.

Short-Sleeve T-Shirt

Pattern pieces
#20, #21, #30

Supplies:
¼ yd. knit fabric
8″ x 1½″ knit ribbing
2″ Velcro strip

Instructions:

1. Cut one front, two backs, and two sleeves from the knit fabric.

2. With right sides together, sew the center back seam to the dot marked on the pattern piece. Serge or zigzag stitch each side of back seam allowance separately, including the unstitched part of the seam. Press the seam allowances open and topstitch the open area of the seam.

3. With right sides together, sew the shoulder seams with a serger or zigzag stitch. Fold the ribbing in half lengthwise with right sides together. Stitch the short ends and turn to the right side. Stretching the ribbing to fit the neckline, serge or zigzag stitch the ribbing to the neckline.

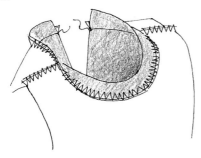

4. Serge or zigzag stitch the lower edges of the sleeves. Press ¼″ to the wrong side and topstitch. With right sides together, serge or zigzag stitch the sleeves to the shirt armholes, easing as necessary.

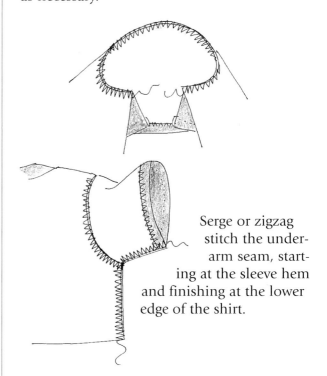

Serge or zigzag stitch the under-arm seam, starting at the sleeve hem and finishing at the lower edge of the shirt.

5. Serge or zigzag stitch the lower edge of the shirt, press the edge ⅜″ to the wrong side, and topstitch.

6. Sew the Velcro to the back opening, lapping right over left.

Pink Top with Capri Pants

The doll shown is a "Dress Me Götz" doll.

*T*his cool little top is perfect for hot summer days. The lined bodice features cut-away armholes with straps. The trim on the front has flat lace zigzag stitched on both sides with a mitered corner at the top. The crocheted butterfly and beaded trim are wonderful embellishment techniques that young girls love.

Capri pants have had many incarnations throughout the last few decades. My mother knew them as "clam diggers," I called them "pedal pushers," and my daughter calls them capri pants. They are a comfortable alternative to long pants in warmer weather, and add another style choice to your wardrobe. These pants have decorative ribbon trim, but can be embellished with machine or hand embroidery, decorative stitches, or appliqués. They are a good project for those learning to sew, as the elastic waist eliminates the set-in waistband and fly.

Pink Top

Pattern pieces #31, #32, #33

Supplies:

¼ yd. pink broadcloth
10" lace insertion (⅜" wide)
½ yd. beaded trim
2" Velcro strip
1 crocheted butterfly

Pink Top

Instructions:

1. Cut two fronts, four backs, and two straps from fabric. Trace the stitching lines for the lace trim onto one of the fronts.

2. Center the lace over the stitching line at the left side of the front. Pin along this line. Miter the corner when you reach the top and pin down the right side. Using a fine zigzag stitch, sew along one side of the lace insertion edge. Repeat with the other side.

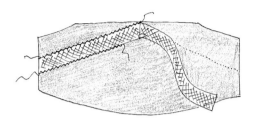

3. With right sides together, stitch the lace-trimmed front to two of the backs. Repeat with the other front and backs (this will be the lining) and set aside.

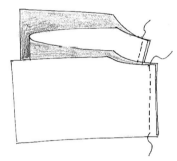

4. Press both long edges of each of the straps ¼" to the wrong side. Fold the straps in half lengthwise so the pressed edges meet and stitch close to the folds.

Pin one end of each strap to the front on the seam line as marked on the pattern piece. Pin the other end to the back on the seam line as marked on the pattern piece. Repeat with the other strap on the other side of the garment. Baste.

5. On the right side, pin the beaded trim to the seam line of the lower edge of the lining. (The trim I used has a ¼" ribbon heading with the strung beads attached to one side.) Using a zipper foot, stitch along the ribbon very close to the beads.

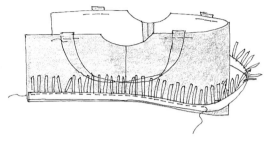

Press the ribbon on the beaded trim to the wrong side. (A small mini-iron works well to press this small seam and avoid pressing the beads.)

6. With right sides together, stitch the lining to the top along each center back and along the top edge. Clip the curves, trim the seam allowances, turn to the right side, and press.

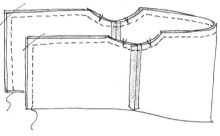

7. Press the lower edge of the top ¼" to the wrong side. Pin it to the lining so the ribbon heading is enclosed and the beads extend out. Stitch close to the pressed edge.

8. Lapping right over left, sew Velcro to the back opening.

9. Tack a crocheted butterfly (see instructions on page 29) to the front as shown in the photograph.

Capri Pants
Pattern piece #34

Supplies:
$\frac{1}{4}$ yd. chambray fabric
11" elastic ($\frac{1}{4}$" wide)
$\frac{1}{2}$ yd. ribbon trim ($\frac{1}{2}$" wide)
1 crocheted butterfly

Instructions:

1. Cut four capri pants from fabric. With right sides together, stitch two pants together at the side seam. Stop stitching at the dot marked on the pattern piece.

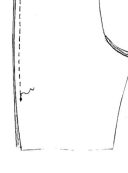

Press the seam allowance open and topstitch the open part of seam. Repeat with the remaining pattern pieces.

2. Serge or zigzag stitch the lower edges of the pants. Press $\frac{1}{2}$" to the wrong side and topstitch.

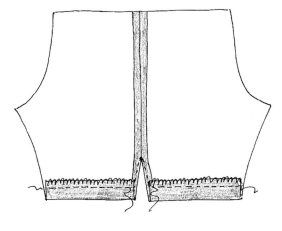

Cut a length of ribbon to fit around the bottom edge of each pant leg plus $\frac{1}{2}$". Pin the ribbon across the pant leg $\frac{1}{4}$" from the folded edge, wrapping the extra $\frac{1}{2}$" of the ribbon to the wrong side of the side seam slit. Zigzag stitch each side of the ribbon to the pants.

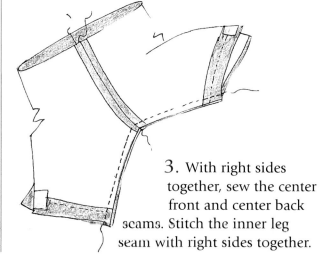

3. With right sides together, sew the center front and center back seams. Stitch the inner leg seam with right sides together.

4. Serge or zigzag stitch the top of the pants. Press the seam ½″ to the wrong side and stitch ⅜″ from the fold, leaving a 1″ opening at the center back to insert the elastic into the casing.

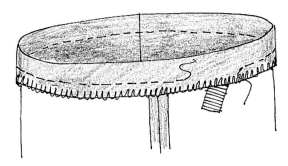

5. Insert the elastic into the casing. Overlap the ends of the elastic and stitch. Stitch the opening closed.

6. Tack a crocheted butterfly (see instructions that follow) to the lower left pant leg as shown in the photograph.

The crocheted butterfly on the pink top.

Crocheted Butterfly

Supplies:
1 ball #8 perle cotton
#7 steel crochet hook

ch = chain stitch
sc = single crochet
dc = double crochet
sl st = slip stitch

Instructions:
Ch 3, join in first ch to make ring.

Round 1: Ch 1, sc 1, chain 4, sc in ring, ch 6, sl st in beginning sc.

Round 2: *Sl st into chain 4 loop, ch 1, 6 sc in loop, sl st in sc of round 1*. Repeat from * to * once more. **Sl st into chain 6 loop, ch 1, 4 sc, sl st in sc of round 1**. Repeat from ** to ** once more. End. Weave in the ends.

Flared Jeans, Quilted Vest, and Bell-Sleeve T-Shirt

These flared jeans are the updated version of the '70s bell-bottoms. Instead of torn knees, they can be decorated many different ways. This pair has decorative braid at the bottom of each pant leg and a colorful dragonfly motif ironed on below the knee. The top of the jeans has a yoke at the front topstitched with brightly colored thread. These pants are suitable for beginners, because there are no pockets.

The short, zipper-front vest is made from pre-quilted fabric. A favorite of the younger set, it can be worn with skirts as well as pants. The zipper may pose a challenge for children, so help may be needed at this point. The collar is optional, which will make the project easier.

The bell sleeves on the t-shirt give it a new look. This shirt uses self-fabric ribbing for the neckline, but a plain ribbing fabric can be used as well.

Flared Jeans
Pattern pieces #19, #35, #36, #37

Supplies:
½ yd. denim fabric
1 decorative snap
Orange topstitching thread
2.0 mm double needle
20" trim (⅝" wide)
5½" elastic (¼" wide)
1 iron-on embroidered motif

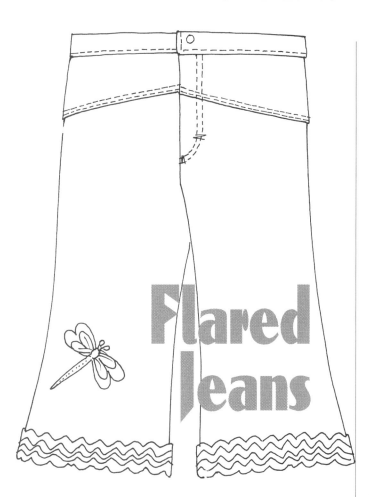

Flared Jeans

Instructions:

1. Cut two front yokes, two fronts, two backs, and one waistband.

2. With right sides together, sew the front yokes to the top edge of the jeans front.

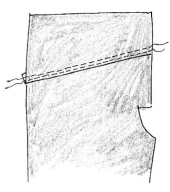

Press the seam allowances toward the top. With top-stitching thread and a double needle, topstitch a scant ⅛" above the seam.

3. With right sides together, sew the fronts at the center seam only up to the dot marked on the pattern piece. Press the right fly edge ⅛" to the wrong side and stitch.

4. Press the left fly toward the wrong side of the jeans along the center front seam line. Stitch along the stitching line marked on the pattern piece, using topstitching thread and a double needle. Stitch the reinforcements on the fly as marked on the pattern piece.

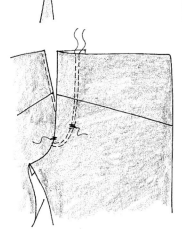

5. With right sides together, sew the center back seam and the side seams.

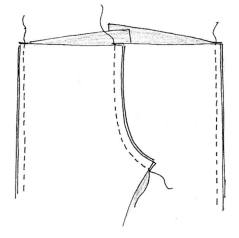

6. Serge or zigzag stitch along one long edge of the waistband.

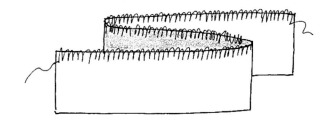

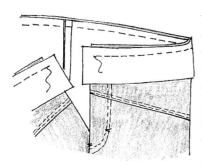

With right sides together, and with the ends extending ¼″ beyond the center fronts of the jeans, sew the long unfinished edge of the waistband to the pants.

Fold the waistband over into the inside of the garment so the waistband is ½″ wide, tucking in the short ends. Topstitch in place, leaving a 1″ opening at each side seam to insert the elastic into the casing. Thread the elastic through the back waistband and secure it at each side seam. Sew the openings closed.

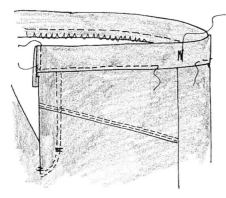

7. Serge or zigzag stitch the lower edges of the jeans. Press the lower edges of the jeans ½″ to the wrong side and stitch. Zigzag stitch the trim to the bottom of each pant leg.

Iron the embroidered motif to the right pant leg where desired.

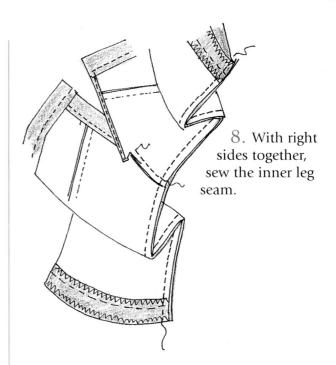

8. With right sides together, sew the inner leg seam.

9. Attach the snap to the ends of the waistband, lapping left over right.

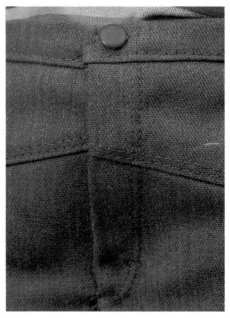

The fly and yoke front on the flared jeans.

32

Quilted Vest

Pattern pieces #38, #39, #40

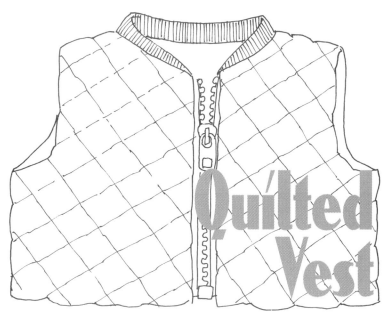

Supplies:

¼ yd. quilted fabric
¼ yd. lining fabric
4″ separating zipper
9″ x 1″ piece of ribbing

Instructions:

1. Cut two fronts and one back from quilted fabric. Cut two fronts and one back from lining fabric. Cut one collar from ribbing.

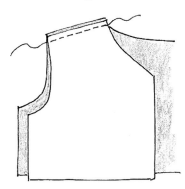

2. With right sides together, sew the fronts to the back at the shoulder seams. Press the seams open. Repeat with the lining pieces and set aside.

3. With right sides together, sew the ends of the ribbing collar. Turn to the right side, keeping the collar folded in half lengthwise.

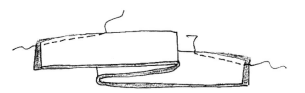

Pin one end of the collar ½″ from the center front edge. Stretch the collar to fit the neckline of the vest until the collar end is ½″ from the other center front edge. Baste.

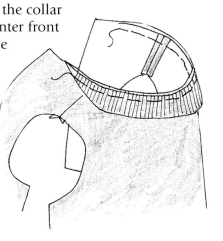

4. Pin the lining to the vest along the neckline, armholes, and front and back lower edges. Stitch.

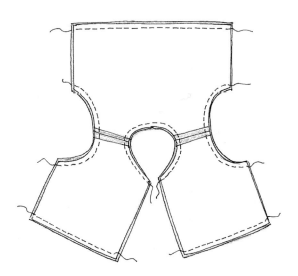

Clip the curves and trim the seam allowances. Turn to the right side through the unsewn side seams. Press.

5. Zigzag stitch or serge the center front edges and press them ½″ to the wrong side. Pin one side of the zipper under the left pressed edge of the vest so the zipper teeth are visible and the zipper pull can slide easily. The bottom of the zipper will be flush with the lower edge of the vest. Fold the fabric at the top of the zipper to the wrong side. Stitch ¼″ from the pressed edge. Repeat with the other side.

6. With right sides together, sew the side seams.

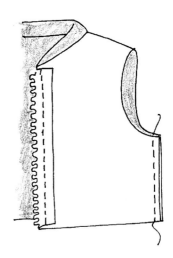

Bell-Sleeve T-Shirt

Pattern pieces
#41, #42, #43

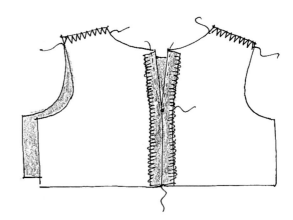

Supplies:
¼ yd. knit fabric
8″ x 1½″ knit ribbing
   (or cut from knit fabric if desired)
2″ Velcro strip

Instructions:

1. Cut one front, two backs, and two sleeves from knit fabric.

2. With right sides together, sew the center back seam to the dot marked on the pattern piece. Serge or zigzag stitch each side of the back seam allowance separately, including the unstitched part of the seam.

Press the seam allowances open and topstitch the open area of the seam.

3. With right sides together, sew the shoulder seams. Fold the ribbing in half lengthwise with the right sides together. Stitch the short ends and turn to the right side. Stretching the ribbing to fit the neck, serge or zigzag stitch the ribbing to the neck opening.

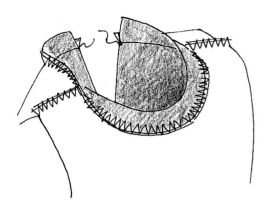

4. Serge or zigzag the bottom of the sleeves. Press ¼" to the wrong side and topstitch. With right sides together, serge or zigzag stitch the sleeves to the shirt armholes.

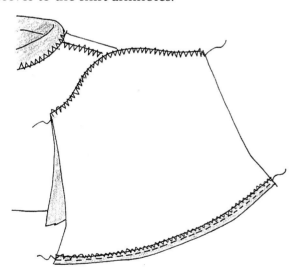

Serge or zigzag stitch the underarm seam, starting at the sleeve hem and finishing at the lower edge of the shirt.

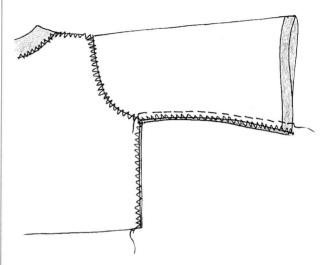

5. Serge or zigzag stitch the lower edge of the shirt and press ⅜" to the wrong side. Topstitch ¼" from the pressed edge.

6. Sew Velcro to the back opening, lapping right over left.

Animal Print Jumper and Cap-Sleeve T-Shirt

*a*nimal prints have been a trend in fashion the last few years and show no sign of declining any time soon. This jumper, with a square neckline and straps, looks great sewn from this tiny pink and black animal print. It is an easy project for children learning to sew.

The cap sleeves of this t-shirt give the shirt a dressier look. This t-shirt is the only one that has no opening in the back, so be sure the knit ribbing is stretchy enough to fit over your doll's head.

Animal Print Jumper
Pattern pieces #44, #45, #46, #47, #48

Supplies:
⅓ yd. animal print fabric
2½" Velcro strip

Instructions:

1. Cut two front yokes, four back yokes, one front skirt, two back skirts, and two straps from fabric.

2. Press each of the long edges of the straps ¼" to the wrong side. Fold the straps in half lengthwise so the folded edges meet. Stitch close to the folded edges on each side of the straps.

3. With right sides together, sew a front yoke to two of the back yokes at the side seams. Repeat with the other front and back yokes to use for the lining. Press the seams open.

4. Pin one end of one of the straps to the front top edge along the seam line ¼" from the left curved armhole edge. Pin the other end of the strap to the back top edge along the seam line ¼" from the left curved armhole edge. Repeat with the other strap and pin to the right front and back. Baste.

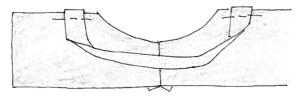

5. With right sides together, sew the yoke lining to the jumper yoke along the center back edges and across the backs, armholes, and front edges.

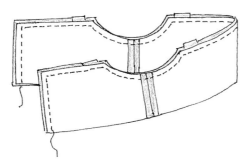

Clip the curves, trim the seam allowances, turn to the right side, and press.

6. Sew the center back seam of the skirt with right sides together to the dot marked on the pattern piece. Press the seam allowances open. Topstitch around the opening above the seam.

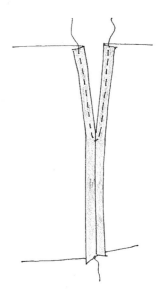

37

7. With right sides together, sew the side seams of the skirt. Stitch the top of the skirt to the lower edge of the yoke, including the yoke lining.

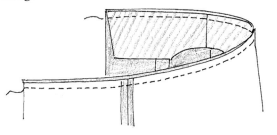

8. Zigzag stitch or serge the lower edge of the jumper skirt. Press the edge ½" to the wrong side. Topstitch ⅜" from the edge.

9. Sew the Velcro strip to the center back edges, lapping right over left.

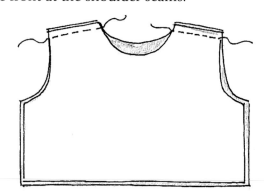

Cap-Sleeve T-Shirt
Pattern pieces #49, #50, #51

Supplies:
¼ yd. knit fabric
8" x 1½" piece of knit ribbing

Instructions:

1. Cut one front, one back, and two sleeves from knit fabric.

2. With right sides together, sew the back to the front at the shoulder seams.

3. Sew the short ends of the ribbing together with right sides together to make a circle. Use pins to mark the half- and quarter-way points around the neck ribbing.

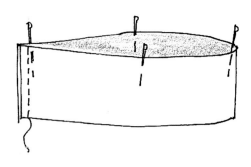

With wrong sides together, fold the ribbing in half lengthwise and pin it to the shirt neckline, stretching the ribbing to fit and matching the pins to the center front, center back, and shoulder seams of the shirt. Stitch.

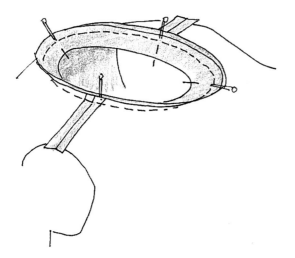

4. Serge or zigzag stitch the bottom edges of the sleeves. Press the edges ¼" to the wrong side and topstitch. Serge or zigzag stitch the sleeve caps to the armholes, easing to fit.

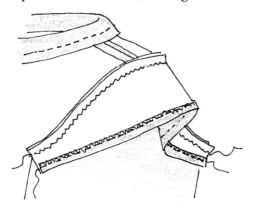

5. With right sides together, serge or zigzag stitch the underarm seam, starting at the sleeve edge and finishing at the lower edge of the shirt.

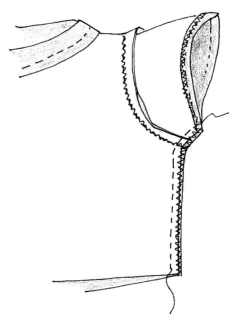

6. Serge or zigzag stitch the lower edge of the shirt and press it ⅜" to the wrong side. Topstitch ¼" from the pressed edge.

Hooded Sweatshirt and Denim Shorts

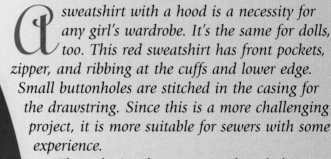

The doll shown is by the Götz Company.

a sweatshirt with a hood is a necessity for any girl's wardrobe. It's the same for dolls, too. This red sweatshirt has front pockets, zipper, and ribbing at the cuffs and lower edge. Small buttonholes are stitched in the casing for the drawstring. Since this is a more challenging project, it is more suitable for sewers with some experience.

These denim shorts are another clothing staple for your doll. They have the same fly as the jeans, but have large square pockets in front. Any sturdy fabric such as twill or poplin can be used instead of denim if you prefer. The shorts are not difficult, but children may want to skip some of the topstitching.

Hooded Sweatshirt
Pattern pieces
#52, #53, #54, #55, #56

Supplies:
½ yd. sweatshirt fleece
3″ ribbing (28″ wide)
6″ separating zipper
⅓ yd. drawstring

Instructions:

1. Cut two fronts, one back, two sleeves, two hoods, and two pockets from sweatshirt fleece. Cut a piece of ribbing 2½″ x 13″ for the jacket waistline, and two 1¼″ x 3½″ pieces for the sleeve cuffs.

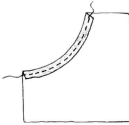

2. Pin the curved edges of the pockets ¼″ to the wrong side and stitch.

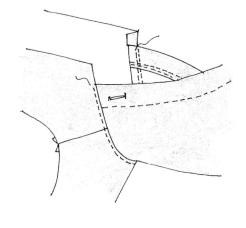

Fold the top and short sides of the pockets to the wrong side and pin them to the sweatshirt front. The long side of the pockets should be flush with the center front of the sweatshirt. The bottom edge of the pockets should be flush with the lower edge of the sweatshirt front. Stitch across the top and short sides of the pockets to attach them to the sweatshirt. Baste the long side and bottom edge to the sweatshirt front.

3. With right sides together, sew the sweatshirt fronts to the back at the shoulder seams.

4. Sew the hood pieces with right sides together along the curved center back seam.

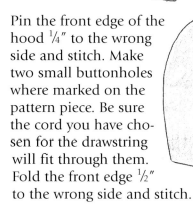

Pin the front edge of the hood ¼″ to the wrong side and stitch. Make two small buttonholes where marked on the pattern piece. Be sure the cord you have chosen for the drawstring will fit through them. Fold the front edge ½″ to the wrong side and stitch.

5. With right sides together, stitch the neck edge of the hood to the neckline of the sweatshirt. (The hood will come approximately ¼″ from the center front edges.) Pin the seam allowances away from the hood and topstitch over them close to the seam.

6. Fold the cuff ribbing in half lengthwise with wrong sides together. Stretch the cuffs to fit the lower edge of the right side of each sleeve and serge or zigzag stitch. Pin the seam allowances to the sleeves and topstitch on the sleeves close to the seam.

7. Gather the sleeve caps and pull the gathering threads to fit the sweatshirt armholes. With right sides together, stitch the sleeves to the armholes. Pin the seam allowances to the sweatshirt fronts and back and topstitch close to the seam.

8. Stitch the underarm seam from the wrist to the bottom edge of the jacket.

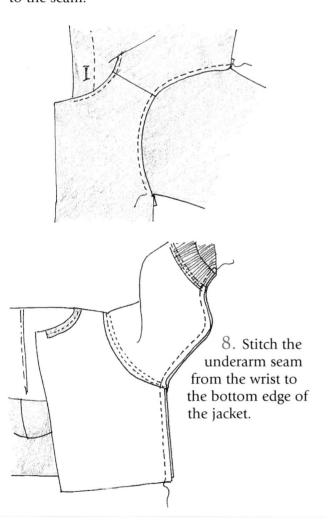

9. Fold the waistline ribbing in half lengthwise with wrong sides together. Serge or zigzag stitch the ribbing to the lower edge of the jacket, stretching the ribbing to fit. Pin the seam allowance to the sweatshirt fronts and back and topstitch close to the seam.

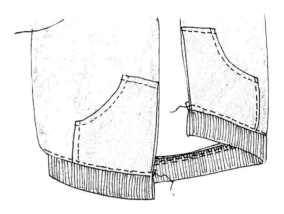

10. Fold the left side of the center front edge (including the ribbing) ¼" to the wrong side and pin it to the left side of the zipper, making sure to leave enough room for the zipper slide to move. Stitch. Repeat with the right side of the zipper.

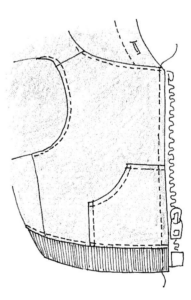

11. Thread the cord for the drawstring through the hood casing. Tie a knot in each end.

Denim Shorts

Pattern pieces #19, #57, #58, #59

Supplies:

¼ yd. denim fabric

5″ elastic (¼″ wide)

1 decorative snap

2.0 double needle

White topstitching thread

Instructions:

1. Cut two fronts, two backs, two pockets, and one waistband from fabric.

2. Press the diagonal side of each pocket ¼″ to the wrong side. Topstitch a scant ⅛″ from the edge with a double needle and topstitching thread.

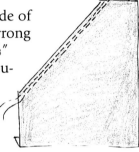

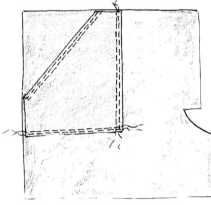

Press the long side and bottom edges of the pockets ¼″ to the wrong side. Place the pockets on each shorts front, keeping the top and short side edges flush with the top and side of each shorts front. Topstitch with the double needle and white thread a scant ⅛″ from the pressed edges of the pocket.

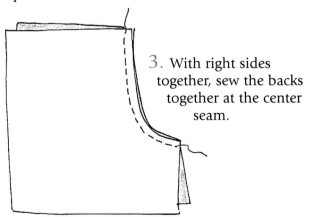

3. With right sides together, sew the backs together at the center seam.

4. With right sides together, sew the fronts at the center seam up to the dot marked on the pattern piece. Press the right fly edge ⅛″ toward the wrong side and stitch.

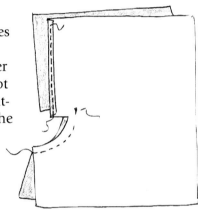

5. Press the left fly toward the wrong side of the pants along the center front seam line. Stitch along the stitching line with a double needle and white thread as marked on the pattern piece. Stitch the reinforcements on the fly as marked on the pattern piece.

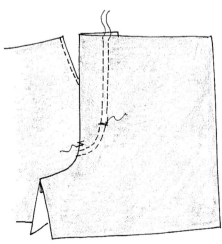

43

6. With right sides together, sew the side seams.

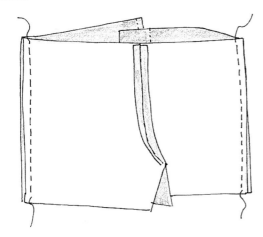

7. Serge or zigzag stitch along one long edge of the waistband. With right sides together, and with ends extending ¼″ beyond the center fronts of the shorts, sew the long unfinished edge of the waistband to the shorts.

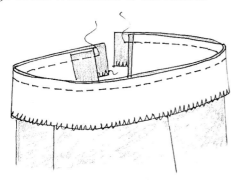

Fold the waistband over to the inside of the garment so the waistband is ½″ wide, tucking in the short ends. Topstitch it in place, leaving a 1″ opening at each side seam to insert the elastic into the casing. Thread the elastic through the back waistband and secure it at each side seam. Sew the openings closed.

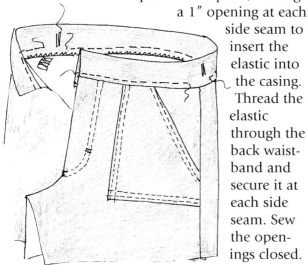

8. Serge or zigzag stitch the lower edges of the shorts. Press this edge ½″ to the wrong side and stitch ¼″ from the pressed edge.

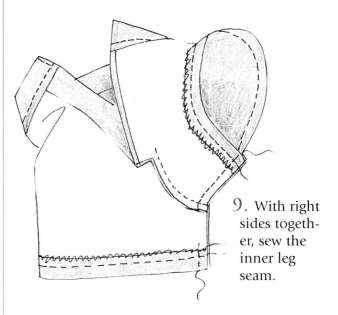

9. With right sides together, sew the inner leg seam.

10. Attach the snap to the ends of the waistband, lapping left over right.

The pocket and fly on the denim shorts.

Long Denim Skirt and V-Neck T-Shirt

The doll shown is by the Götz Company.

$\mathscr{C}$asual wear today should include a long, straight denim skirt. This one sewn from white denim has front pockets, a fly front opening, and topstitching on the front seams. Like the jeans in this collection, it has elastic in the back waistband to insure proper fit. Aside from the topstitching, it is suitable for young sewers.

The lemon yellow t-shirt has a v-neck, making it one of the easiest t-shirts in the collection. The neckline is simply serged or zigzag stitched, pressed to the wrong side, and topstitched. The sleeves stop just below the elbow for a very contemporary look.

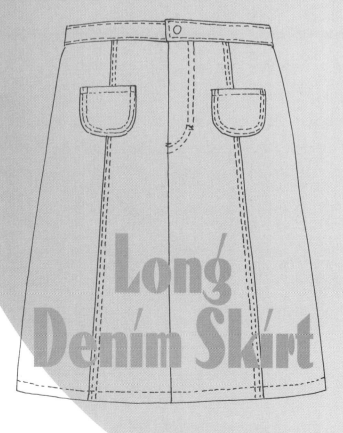

Long Denim Skirt

Long Denim Skirt
Pattern pieces
#60, #61, #62, #63, #64

Supplies:
½ yd. lightweight denim
1 decorative snap or button
4½" elastic (¼" wide)
2.0 mm double needle
Topstitching thread

Instructions:

1. Cut two fronts, two side fronts, two pockets, two backs, and one waistband.

2. With right sides together, stitch one front to a side front. Repeat with the other front and side front.

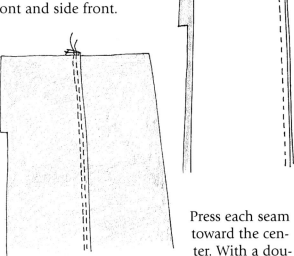

Press each seam toward the center. With a double needle and topstitching thread, stitch a scant ⅛" away from each seam on the front skirt piece.

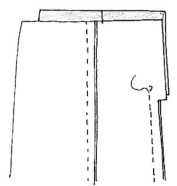

3. Stitch the center front seam only up to the dot marked on the pattern piece.

Press the right fly edge ⅛" toward the wrong side and stitch. Press the left fly toward the wrong side of the skirt along the center front seam line. Stitch along the stitching line marked on the pattern piece. Stitch the reinforcements on the fly as marked on the pattern piece.

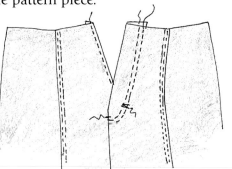

The pocket and top-stitched seams on the denim skirt.

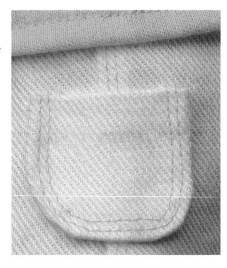

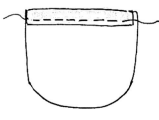

4. Press the top edge of the pockets ¼" to the wrong side and stitch.

Press the curved edges of pockets ¼" to the wrong side. Pin the pockets over the side front seams 1⅜" from the top edge of the skirt. With a double needle and topstitching thread, stitch around each pocket ⅛" from the pressed edges.

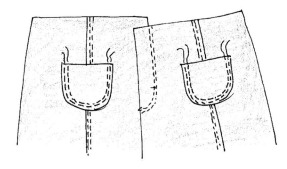

5. With right sides together, sew the center back seam of the skirt. Sew the back to the front at the side seams.

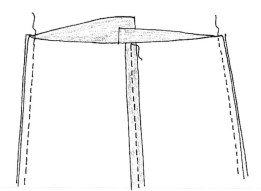

6. Press one long edge of the waistband ¼" to the wrong side. Pin the right side of the other long edge of the waistband to the wrong side of the skirt, extending the short ends ¼" beyond the front edges. Stitch.

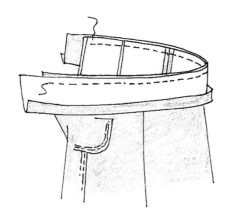

Fold the waistband over to the right side and pin, tucking in the short ends. Leaving a 1" opening at each side seam, stitch around all sides of the waistband a scant ⅛" from each edge with top-stitching thread. Thread the elastic through the back casing and secure the ends. Sew the opening closed.

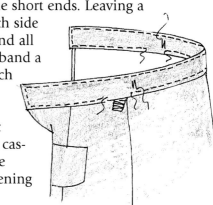

7. Serge or zigzag stitch around the hem of the skirt and press ½" to the wrong side. Stitch ⅜" from the pressed edge.

8. Apply a decorative snap to the front waistband ends, lapping left over right.

V-Neck T-Shirt

Pattern pieces
#65, #66, #67

Supplies:
¼ yd. t-shirt knit fabric
2½" strip Velcro

Instructions:

1. Cut one front, two backs, and two sleeves.

2. Sew the backs together at the center back seam up to the dot marked on the pattern piece.

Press the seam allowances open and topstitch around the opening.

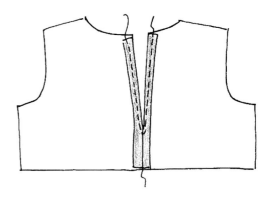

47

3. With right sides together, sew the front to the backs at the shoulder seams.

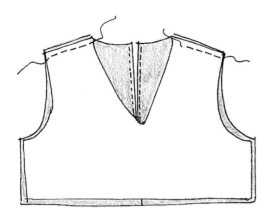

4. Serge or zigzag stitch around the neckline. Press the neck edge $\frac{1}{4}''$ to the wrong side and topstitch.

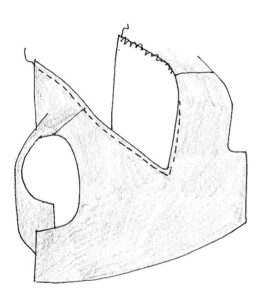

5. Serge or zigzag stitch the lower edges of the sleeves. Press the edges $\frac{1}{4}''$ to the wrong side and topstitch.

6. With right sides together, sew the sleeves to the armholes, easing as necessary.

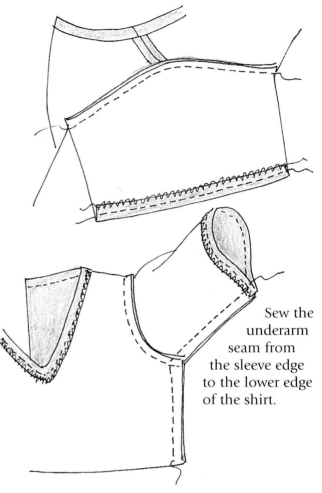

Sew the underarm seam from the sleeve edge to the lower edge of the shirt.

7. Serge or zigzag stitch the hem of the shirt. Press $\frac{1}{4}''$ to the wrong side and topstitch.

8. Sew Velcro to the back opening, lapping right over left.

Outerwear

Coat with Crocheted Posies and Pull-On Pants

*E*very doll needs a warm coat, especially one with contrasting piping, covered buttons, and brightly colored crocheted flowers for decoration on the pockets. I made this coat from one of the new faux suede fabrics available. They are easy to sew since they are knitted and do not ravel. The buttons are sewn on top of the right side of the coat with snaps underneath, but you may choose to work buttonholes on your garment. Children will be able to stitch the major seams of the coat, but may need assistance with the curves of the collar.

These pull-on pants are perfect for beginning sewers. The waistband is all one piece with elastic in the back. It is a quick project that looks great in a variety of medium weight fabrics, such as twill, denim, poplin, or corduroy.

Coat with Crocheted Posies
Pattern pieces #68, #69, #70, #71, #72, #73

Supplies:
$1/3$ yd. faux suede fabric
$1/3$ yd. lining fabric
$1\frac{1}{4}$ yd. contrasting piping
3 buttons ($7/16''$) to cover, or matching buttons
3 snaps
6 crochet flower embellishments

Instructions:

1. Cut two fronts, one back, two collars, two sleeves, four cuffs, and two pockets from suede fabric. Cut two fronts and one back from lining fabric.

2. Press the top edge of each pocket ¼″ to the wrong side and stitch. Sew piping along the seam allowance of the curved edge of the pockets, extending the ends of the piping slightly.

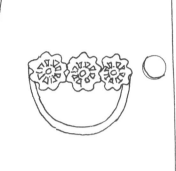

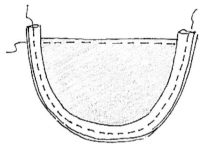

Press the seam allowance to the wrong side so the piping is on the outer edge of each pocket. Pin the pockets to the coat where marked on the pattern piece, tucking under the piping ends. Stitch the pockets to the coat along the pocket/piping seam.

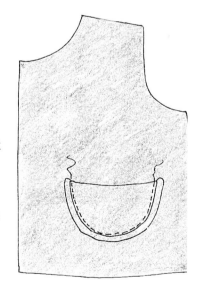

3. With right sides together, sew the fronts to the back at the shoulder seams. Press the seam allowances open. Repeat with the lining and set aside.

4. Sew piping along the seam allowance on the outer curved edge of one of the collars. With right sides together, sew the other collar to the collar with piping. Clip the curves, turn to the right side, and press.

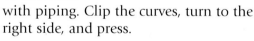

5. Pin the lined collar to the right side of the neckline edge, matching the center back fold lines. Note that the collar does not extend all the way to the center front. Baste.

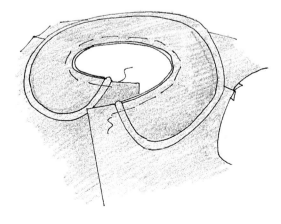

6. With right sides together, pin the coat lining to the coat. Sew around the neckline, down the center fronts, and across each lower front and back edge.

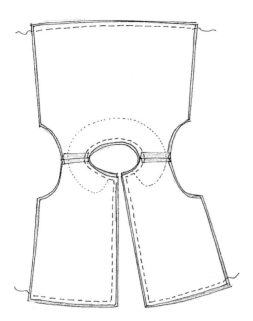

Clip the curves and corners, trim the seam allowances, and turn it to the right side. Press.

7. Sew piping along the seam allowance on the right side of the longer straight edge of each cuff. With right sides together, sew a second cuff to the cuff with piping.

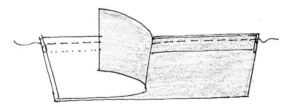

Turn it to the right side and press. With the right side of the cuff to the wrong side of the sleeve edge, sew the cuffs to the sleeves. Fold the cuff up over the sleeve and press. Baste the cuffs to the sleeves along the side seams.

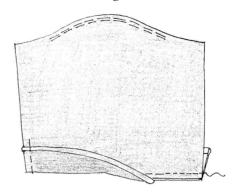

8. Gather the sleeve caps slightly. Pin the sleeve into the armhole, easing as needed. Stitch. With right sides together, sew the under-arm seams from the cuff to the hem of the coat.

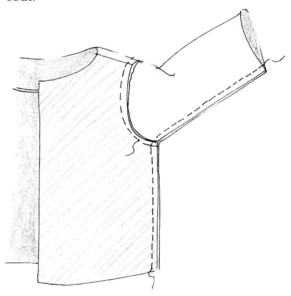

9. Sew the buttons to the right side of the front of the coat where marked on the pattern piece. Sew one half of a snap under each button and the other half to the left side of the coat.

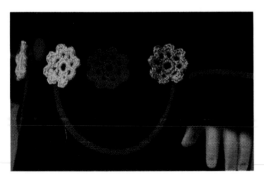

Crocheted Posies

Supplies:
1 ball of #8 perle cotton in three colors
#7 steel crochet hook

ch = chain stitch   dc = double crochet
sc = single crochet   sl st = slip stitch

Instructions:

With 1 color of perle cotton, ch 5, join in first ch to make ring.

Round 1: Ch 1, 8 sc in ring, sl st into first sc.

Round 2: Ch 1, sc in first sc, 3 ch, sc in each sc of round 1. Sl st into base of first loop - 8 loops.

Round 3: Sl st into first loop, ch 1, sc, 3 dc, sc in each loop. Sl st into base of first sc. End. Weave in the ends.

Make another posy in the same color of perle cotton. Make two more posies in each of the remaining colors of perle cotton. Tack each of the posies to the top of each pocket as shown in the photograph.

Pull-On Pants

Pattern pieces #74, #75, #76

Supplies:

⅓ yd. poplin or twill fabric
5½" elastic (¼" wide)

Instructions:

1. Cut two fronts, two backs, and one waist-band from fabric.

2. With right sides together, sew the center front and back seams. Clip the curves and press.

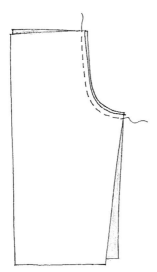

3. With right sides together, sew the fronts to the backs at the side seams.

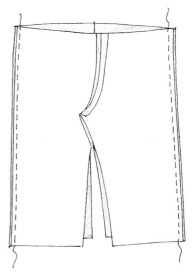

4. Serge or zigzag stitch the lower edge of each pant leg. Press this ⅜" to the wrong side. Topstitch ¼" from the pressed edge.

5. Sew the inner leg seam with right sides together.

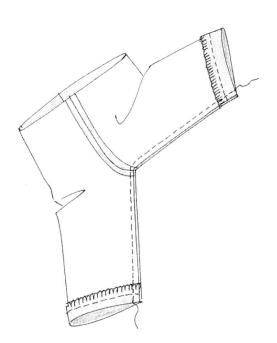

6. With right sides together, pin the short ends of the waistband together, forming a circle. Stitch and press the seam allowances open.

7. Serge or zigzag stitch along one long edge of the waistband. Sew the right side of the unstitched edge to the right side of the top edge of the pants, matching the waistband seam to center back seam of the pants.

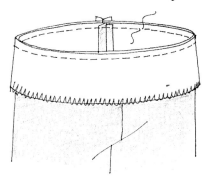

8. Fold the waistband over into the inside of the garment so the waistband is ½" wide. Pin it carefully and topstitch from the right side, leaving a 1" opening at each side seam to insert the elastic.

9. Thread the elastic through the back waistband and secure it at each side seam with a few machine stitches. Stitch the openings closed.

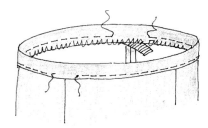

Fleece Jacket and Nylon Wind Pants

*F*leece is a wonderful new fabric for outer-wear. Dolls want to get in on the action, too, with their own cozy jacket. This jacket has a zippered front and a collar to protect from the cold. The pockets are large, with zippers to keep them closed, just like in human jackets. Look for small prints that are suitable for dolls and then you can coordinate accessories from the colors in the print. The pockets with zippers can be eliminated for beginning sewers if necessary.

The nylon pants can be made from any windproof fabric if your doll will be out in the cold. They can also be made from sweatshirt fleece or any medium weight fabric. Children will find the pants a good beginning project.

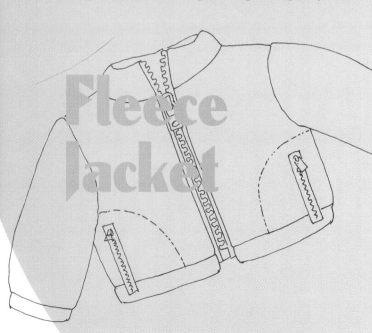

The doll shown is from the Springfield Collection by Fibre-Craft Materials Corp.

Fleece Jacket

Fleece Jacket
Pattern pieces #77, #78, #79, #80, #81

Supplies:
⅓ yd. fleece fabric
6″ separating zipper
21½″ elastic (¼″ wide)
2 zippers (2″)

Instructions:

1. Cut two fronts, one back, two sleeves, two pockets, and one collar from fleece fabric.

2. Cut a slit in each front where marked on the pattern piece. Fold one long edge of the slit ¼" to the wrong side and pin the zipper underneath. Fold the other side to the wrong side and pin to the zipper. The zipper pull and teeth should be fully exposed. Stitch around all sides of the zipper close to the fold.

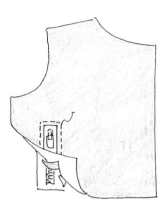

3. Pin each pocket on the wrong side of the jacket so the straight edges of the pocket are flush with the sides and bottom edges of the jacket fronts. Stitch each pocket to the jacket fronts very close to the curved edge of the pocket.

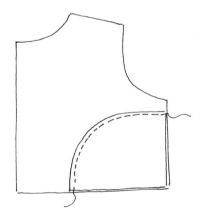

4. With right sides together, sew the fronts to the back at the shoulder seams.

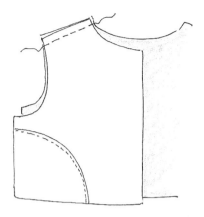

5. With right sides together, sew one long edge of the collar to the neck edge of the jacket.

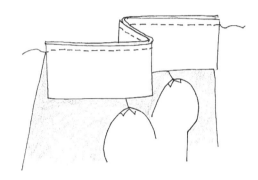

Pin one side of the center front edge of the jacket (including the collar) ½" to the wrong side. Place the bottom half of the zipper under the folded edge 1¼" from the lower edge of the jacket, keeping the zipper teeth fully exposed. (The zipper will only extend up approximately half the collar width. If the zipper fabric extends beyond that, trim off the excess.) Stitch ¼" from the folded edge from the top of the collar to the lower edge of the jacket. Repeat with the other side of the jacket and the other half of the zipper.

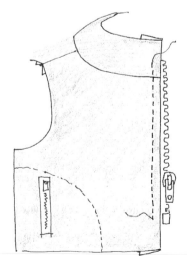

6. Fold the collar in half widthwise. Turn the long edge and both short ends ¼" to the wrong side and pin, tucking in the collar/jacket seam allowance. Stitch ¼" from the folded edges.

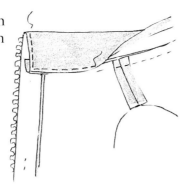

7. Fold the lower sleeve edges ¼" to the wrong side. Fold another ½" to form a casing. Stitch close to the fold. Cut 4" of elastic for each sleeve and thread it through the casing. Secure at each side.

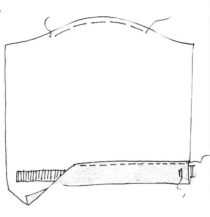

Gather the sleeve caps slightly. With right sides together, pin the sleeves to the armholes, easing as necessary. Stitch.

8. Sew the underarm seams from the sleeve edge to the lower edge of the jacket.

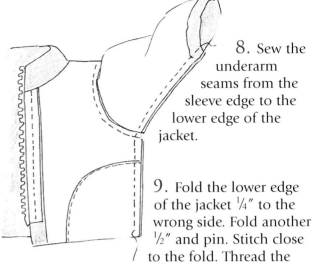

9. Fold the lower edge of the jacket ¼" to the wrong side. Fold another ½" and pin. Stitch close to the fold. Thread the remaining elastic through the casing and secure at each center front.

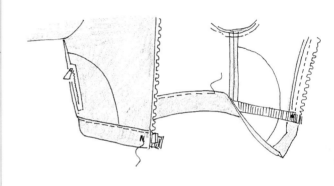

Nylon Wind Pants
Pattern piece #82

Supplies:
½ yd. windproof nylon fabric
1½ yd. ribbon (¼" wide)
21" elastic (¼" wide)

Instructions:
1. Cut four from the pattern piece. (The backs and fronts are cut from the same pattern piece.)

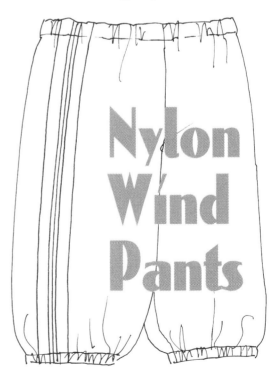

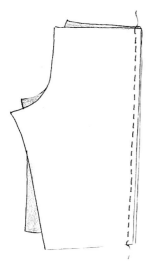

2. With the right sides together, stitch each front to a back at the side seams.

Press open. Pin the ribbon a scant ⅛″ away from the left side of one of the seam lines from the waist to the ankle. Zigzag stitch along both sides of the ribbon. Cut off the excess. Pin the ribbon to the right side of the side seam a scant ⅛″ from the edge and stitch. Repeat with the other side seam on the other pants half.

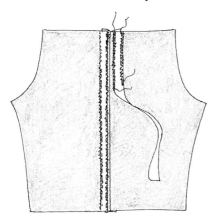

3. With right sides together, sew the fronts together at the center front seam and the backs together at the center back seam.

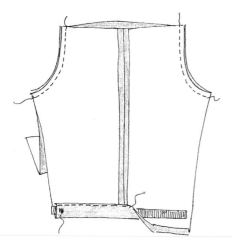

4. Press the lower edges of each pant leg ¼″ to the wrong side. Press again another ½″ and stitch close to the fold. Cut the remaining elastic in half and thread each piece through each leg and secure as before.

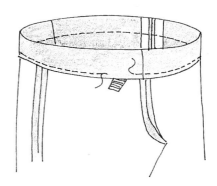

5. Press the waistline edge ¼″ to the wrong side. Press again another ½″ and stitch close to the fold, leaving a 1″ opening at the back. Thread an 11″ piece of elastic through the waistline casing and secure it with machine stitching at the center back. Stitch the opening closed.

6. With right sides together, sew the inner leg seam.

Sleepwear

59

Flannel Pajamas

*C*lassic flannel pajamas are warm, cozy, and always in fashion. This style features heart-shaped buttons and piping on the contrasting pocket, collar, and cuffs. The pants have a simple elastic waistband, so children can help make their doll's pajamas.

Supplies:

⅔ yd. plaid flannel

¼ yd. contrasting flannel for collar, pocket, and cuffs

⅔ yd. piping

11″ elastic (¼″ wide)

5 buttons (⅜″)

5 snaps

Pajama Top

Pattern pieces
#83, #84, #85, #86, #87, #88, #89

Instructions:

1. Cut two fronts, one back, two sleeves, and two facings from plaid flannel. Cut two collars, two cuffs, and one pocket from contrasting flannel.

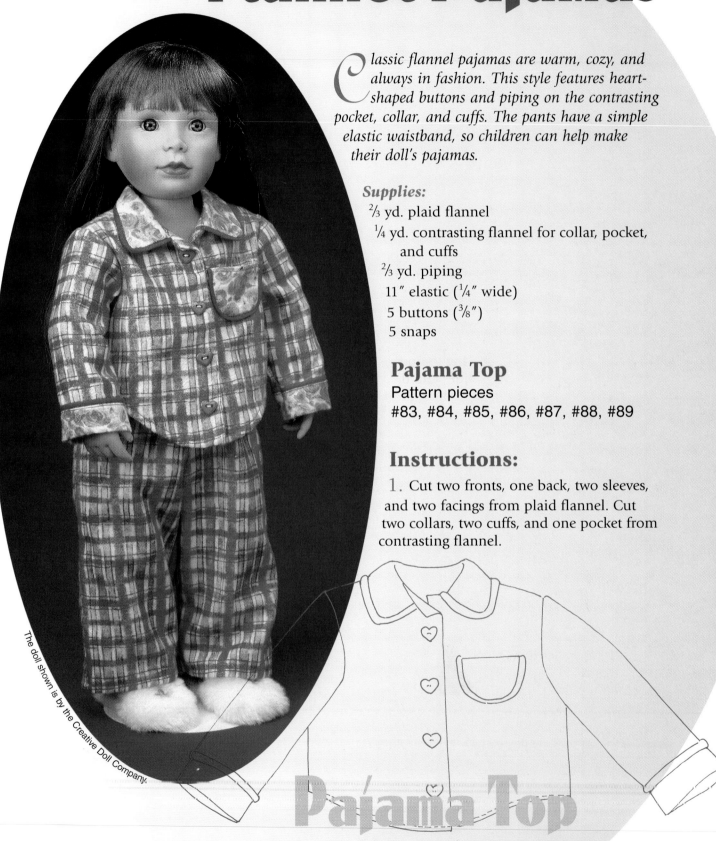

Pajama Top

2. Press the top edge of the pocket ¼" to the wrong side and stitch. Sew piping to the remaining sides of the pocket along the seam line, leaving approximately ¼" of piping at each end.

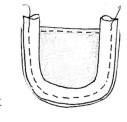

Press the seam allowance to the wrong side. Tuck the piping ends to the wrong side and stitch the pocket to the top as marked on the pattern piece along the piping seam line.

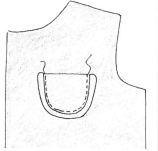

3. With right sides together, sew the backs to the front at the shoulder seams.

4. Sew the piping to both short sides and the outside edge of the right side of the collar along the seam line, clipping the seam allowance of the piping as you turn the corners.

5. Put the collars right sides together and stitch along the seam line on the same three sides as you stitched the piping. Clip the corners, turn to the right side, and press.

6. With right sides together, center the collar along the neckline of the top. The collar does not go all the way to the center front edges. Stitch.

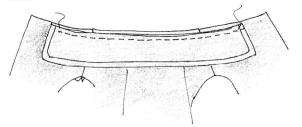

7. Sew the center back seam of the facings with right sides together. Press open. To clean finish the outside edge, serge or zigzag stitch around the edge.

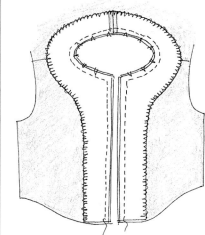

Pin the facing to the center fronts and the neckline and stitch.

Clip the curves, trim the seam allowances, and press to the right side. Understitch the facing to the pajama top close to the neckline to anchor the facing. This will not show when the collar is laid back down again.

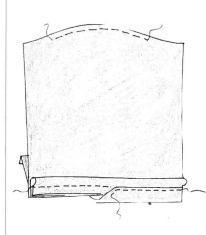

8. Stitch piping to the lower edge of each sleeve. Stitch the right side of the cuff to the wrong side of the sleeve. Fold the cuff over to the right side and stitch close to the folded edge.

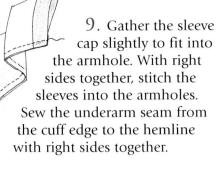

9. Gather the sleeve cap slightly to fit into the armhole. With right sides together, stitch the sleeves into the armholes. Sew the underarm seam from the cuff edge to the hemline with right sides together.

10. Serge or zigzag stitch the hem of the pajama top. Press this edge ¼" to the wrong side and topstitch.

11. Sew four evenly spaced buttons to the right side of the pajama top front. Sew one snap half under each button and the other snap half to the other side of the top.

Pajama Bottoms
Pattern piece #90

Instructions:

1. Cut four pajama bottoms from plaid flannel. With right sides together, stitch the center front and back seams.

2. Stitch the front to the back at the side seams with right sides together.

3. Hem the pajama bottoms by pressing the edge ¼" to the wrong side. Press again another ¼" and stitch.

4. Press the top edge of the pajama bottoms ¼" to the wrong side. Press again another ½" and stitch close to the fold, leaving a 1" opening near the back seam. Insert elastic into the casing and secure the ends by overlapping slightly. Stitch the opening closed.

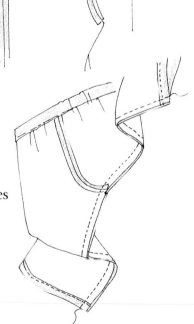

5. With right sides together, sew the inner leg seam.

Tank Top and Boxer Shorts

*O*ne of the most popular shirt styles for girls today is the tank top. This miniaturized version is made from a knit with a waffle-like texture. The straps are bands of the knit fabric. The tank top can be decorated many different ways, such as embroidery or decorative stitches. To make this tank top look like nightwear, I used lace trim and ribbons across the top edge in front.

The boxer shorts are very versatile. They can be made from flannel or many adorable small prints and be worn for bedtime or playtime. Children will easily be able to make them for their dolls.

Tank Top

Pattern pieces #91, #92

Supplies:

¼ yd. knit fabric

4″ lace galloon trim (lace trim that has scalloped edges on both sides with holes for ribbon in the center)

⅓ yd. satin ribbon (¼″ wide)

3″ Velcro strip

The doll shown is by the Götz Company.

Instructions:

1. Cut one front, two backs, and two 1" x 8" strips from knit fabric (cut the two strips on the bias if the knit fabric is quite stable).

2. Fold the top edges of the front and each back ¼" to the wrong side and stitch with a narrow zigzag stitch. Fold the center back edges ¼" to the wrong side and stitch with a narrow zigzag stitch.

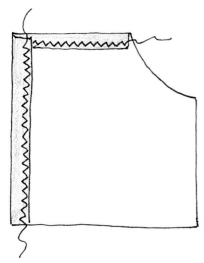

3. Weave ribbon through the beading of the lace galloon and cut off the excess ribbon. Place the galloon lace trim over the stitching on the front. Stitch in place with a narrow zigzag stitch on both sides of the ribbon.

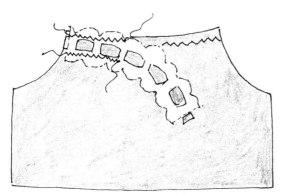

4. Pin the right side of one of the strips to the wrong side of one of the front armholes, beginning at the side seam. When you reach the top, measure 3" of the strip and mark. Resume pinning the strip to the back armhole at this mark

and pin around the rest of the armhole. Stitch with a narrow zigzag stitch.

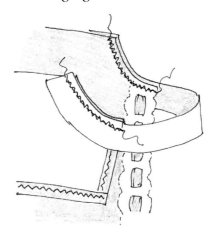

5. Fold the strip over to the right side of the front and back armholes, tucking the raw edge ¼" to the wrong side. On the 3" strap area, fold both of the raw edges ¼" to the wrong side and fold again so these folded edges meet. Pin securely and stitch with a narrow zigzag stitch. Repeat with the other armhole.

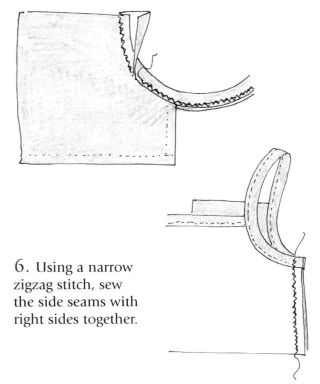

6. Using a narrow zigzag stitch, sew the side seams with right sides together.

7. Lapping right over left, sew Velcro to the center back opening.

8. Tie a bow with the remaining ribbon and tack it to the center of the lace trim.

Boxer Shorts
Pattern piece #93

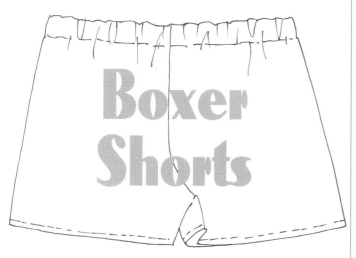

Supplies:
¼ yd. cotton print fabric
11″ elastic (¼″ wide)

Instructions:

1. Cut four shorts from the boxer shorts pattern piece.

2. With right sides together, stitch the center front and back seams.
If desired, stitch the "fake fly" onto the left front as marked on the pattern piece.

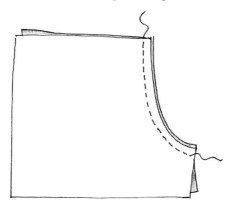

3. Stitch the side seams with right sides together.

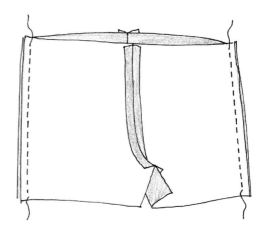

4. Serge or zigzag stitch the top edge of the shorts. Press this edge ½″ to the wrong side. Topstitch ⅜″ from the pressed edge, leaving a 1″ opening at the center back for the casing. Thread elastic through the casing and stitch the ends together, overlapping slightly. Stitch the opening closed.

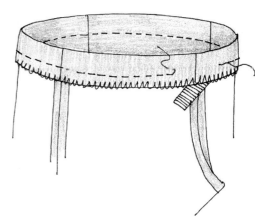

5. Serge or zigzag stitch the hem edges of the shorts. Press this edge ¼″ to the wrong side and topstitch.

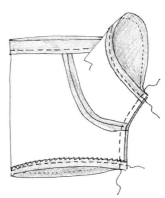

6. With right sides together, sew the inner leg seam.

Sleep Shirt

A sleep shirt is simply a lengthened t-shirt with a curved bottom. This one is made from a small print fabric knit with matching ribbing. Be aware that the shirt does not have an opening in the back, so be sure that your ribbing is stretchy enough to fit over a doll's head. This would be a good project for beginners on the serger, but can be sewn on the sewing machine as well.

Sleep Shirt
Pattern pieces #94, #95, #96

Supplies:
1/3 yd. t-shirt knit fabric
8″ x 1½″ piece of knit ribbing

Instructions:

1. Cut one front, one back, and two sleeves from knit fabric.

2. Serge or zigzag stitch the raw edge of the front from the armhole, around the curved hem, and stopping at the other armhole. Do not cut any fabric from the seam allowance as you stitch. Repeat with the back. With right sides together, sew the back to the front at the shoulder seams using a narrow zigzag stitch or a serged seam.

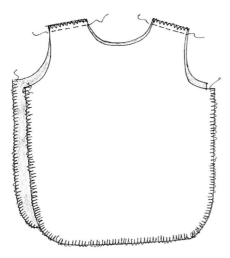

3. Make a circle of the contrasting neckline ribbing and stitch the short ends with right sides together. Use pins to mark the half- and quarter-way points around the ribbing. With wrong sides together, fold the ribbing in half lengthwise and pin it to the sleep shirt neckline, stretching the ribbing to fit. Match the pins to the center front, center back, and shoulder seams of the shirt. Serge or zigzag stitch.

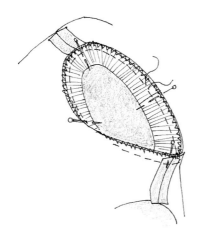

4. Serge or zigzag stitch the lower edges of the sleeves. Press ¼" to the wrong side and topstitch.

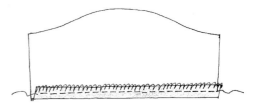

With right sides together, serge or zigzag stitch the sleeves to the shirt armholes.

5. Stitch the underarm seam, beginning at the sleeve edge and stopping at the dot marked on the front and back pattern pieces. Press the seams open.

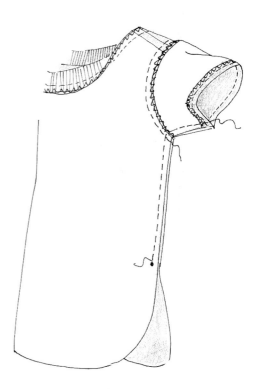

6. Press the curved lower edge ⅜" to the wrong side. Topstitch around the hem.

Special Occasions

A-Line Dress

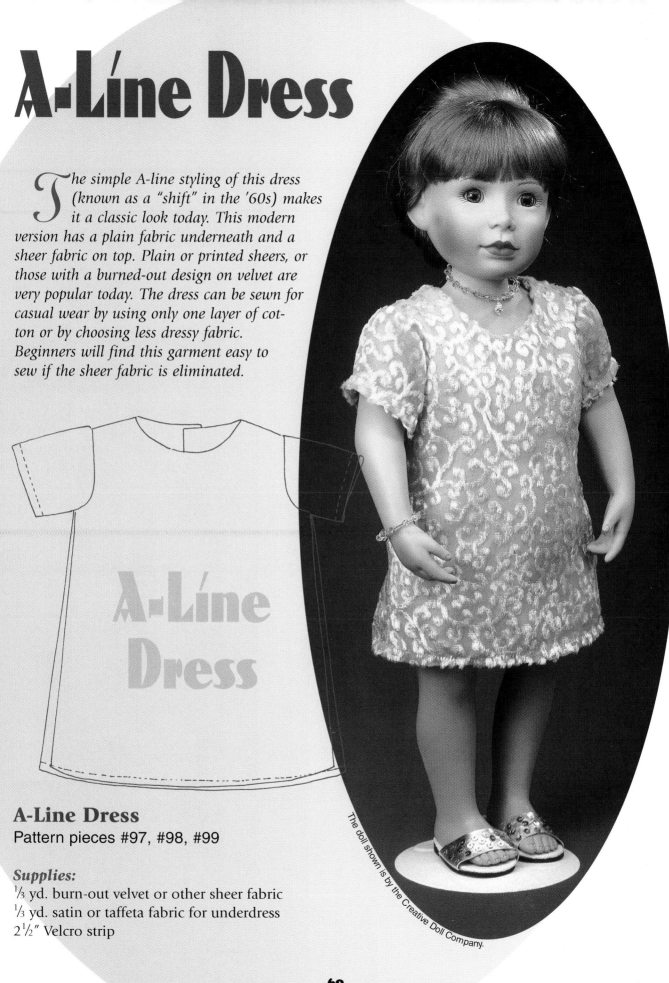

*T*he simple A-line styling of this dress (known as a "shift" in the '60s) makes it a classic look today. This modern version has a plain fabric underneath and a sheer fabric on top. Plain or printed sheers, or those with a burned-out design on velvet are very popular today. The dress can be sewn for casual wear by using only one layer of cotton or by choosing less dressy fabric. Beginners will find this garment easy to sew if the sheer fabric is eliminated.

A-Line Dress

A-Line Dress
Pattern pieces #97, #98, #99

Supplies:
⅓ yd. burn-out velvet or other sheer fabric
⅓ yd. satin or taffeta fabric for underdress
2½" Velcro strip

The doll shown is by the Creative Doll Company.

Instructions:

1. Cut out one front and two backs from the satin. Cut one front, two backs, two sleeves, and a bias strip 1″ x 10¼″ from sheer fabric.

2. With right sides together, stitch the center back seam from the hemline to the dot marked on the pattern piece. Repeat with the sheer fabric.

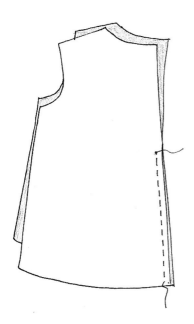

3. Place the wrong side of the sheer fabric over the right side of the satin on the front and backs. Baste across the shoulder seam of each piece to prevent shifting. Stitch the shoulder seams with right sides together.

4. Pin both fabrics of the open area of the center back seam together and baste close to the fabric edges. Press the seam ¼″ to the wrong side and topstitch around the opening.

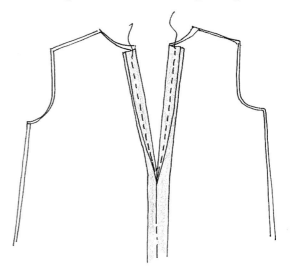

5. Press one long side of the bias strip ¼″ to the wrong side. Pin the other side of the strip to the neckline of the dress, extending both ends of the strip ¼″ beyond the center back seam. Stitch. Fold the strip to the inside and stitch, enclosing both ends. (If you don't want the stitching to show on the right side, slip-stitch the bias to the dress by hand.)

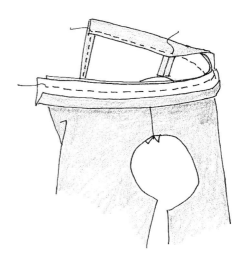

6. Press the lower edge of the sleeve ¼″ to the wrong side. Press again another ¼″ and stitch. (You may choose to use a narrow hem foot to hem the sleeves.)

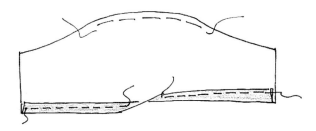

Gather the top of the sleeve and pull the threads to gather the sleeve cap slightly. With right sides together, stitch the sleeve to the armhole. Repeat with the other sleeve.

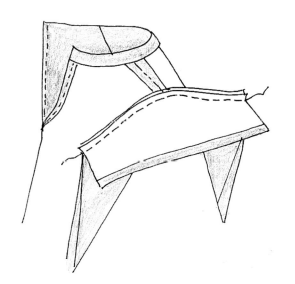

7. With right sides together, stitch the underarm seams from the sleeve edge to the armhole seam only.

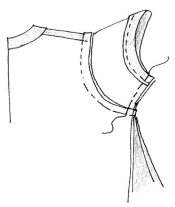

Stitch the sheer fabric side seams together after moving the satin fabric away from the seam line. Stitch the satin fabric side seams together after moving the sheer fabric away from the seam line. Press.

8. Serge or zigzag stitch the hem edge of each layer of dress. Press each one ¼″ to the wrong side and topstitch.

9. Lapping right over left, sew Velcro to the center back opening.

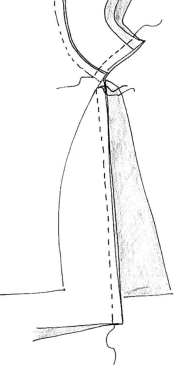

Long Circle Skirt and Crushed Velvet Top

The doll shown is by the Götz Company.

*D*olls will be ready for any special occasion when they wear this outfit. The floor-length skirt has a sheer overlay and set-on waistband. By eliminating the sheer layer, the skirt is an appropriate project for children.

The top is made from crushed velvet, a knitted fabric, so it is very easy to sew on. The crushed velvet gives it a formal look, but any knit fabric will work. This is also a good project for beginners.

Long Circle Skirt
Pattern pieces #100, #101, #102

Supplies:
½ yd. satin
½ yd. iridescent organza
1 hook-and-eye closure

Long Circle Skirt

4. Repeat Steps 2 and 3 with the organza skirt. Pin the wrong side of the organza skirt to the right side of the satin skirt. Baste along the waistline.

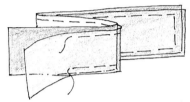

5. Place the wrong side of the organza waistband over the right side of the satin waistband. Baste along all the edges to avoid shifting.

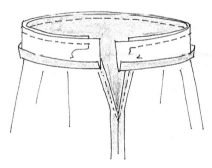

Press one long edge ¼" to the wrong side. Pin the right side of the waistband to the wrong side of the skirt, extending both short ends ¼" beyond the center back edges. Stitch.

Fold the waistband over to the right side and stitch it in place, tucking in the short ends.

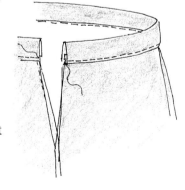

6. Serge or zigzag stitch the hem of the satin skirt. Press this edge ¼" to the wrong side and stitch. Repeat with the organza skirt hem.

7. Sew the hook-and-eye to the waistband, lapping right over left.

Instructions:

1. Cut one front and two backs from the satin. Cut one front and two backs from the organza. Cut the waistband from both the satin and the organza.

2. With right sides together, stitch the center back seam of the satin skirt to the dot marked on the pattern piece. Press the seam open. Topstitch around the opening.

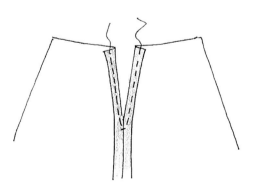

3. Stitch the side seams with right sides together.

Crushed Velvet Top
Pattern pieces #103, #104

Supplies:
¼ yd. crushed velvet fabric
3″ Velcro strip

Instructions:

1. Cut one front and two backs from fabric. Pin the center back edges ¼″ to the wrong side and stitch.

2. With right sides together, serge or zigzag stitch the front to the backs at the shoulder seams.

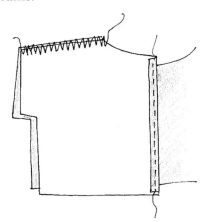

Pin the neckline edge ¼″ to the wrong side and stitch with a narrow zigzag. Pin the sleeve hem edges ¼″ to the wrong side and stitch with a narrow zigzag.

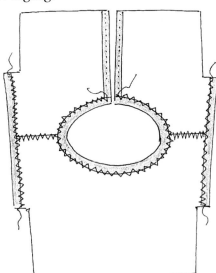

3. Pin the side seams with right sides together. Serge or zigzag stitch, being sure to make a right angle at the armhole. Clip the seams at the right angle and turn to the right side.

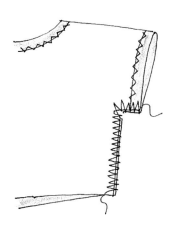

4. Pin the hem of the top ¼″ to the wrong side and topstitch.

5. Sew Velcro to the back opening, lapping right over left.

Sleeveless Party Dress and Velveteen Jacket

*P*arties require special clothes, and this ensemble is perfect. The dress has a sleeveless, lined bodice and a circle skirt. The skirt allows fullness without gathers. The dress can be more casual if sewn in a pretty cotton print. Children will enjoy making this dress but they will need a little assistance with the lining.

The short jacket with a curved front opening adds an elegant touch and is simple to make. The velveteen may pose a bit of a challenge to inexperienced sewers. Using a fabric without a nap will alleviate the problem.

The doll shown is a "Dress Me Götz" doll.

Sleeveless Party Dress

Pattern pieces #105, #106, #107, #108

Supplies:
½ yd. satin fabric
1½" Velcro strip

3. Place the bodice and lining right sides together. Stitch up each center back, around the neckline, and each armhole.

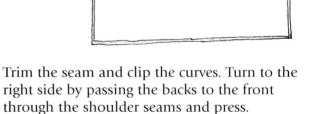

Trim the seam and clip the curves. Turn to the right side by passing the backs to the front through the shoulder seams and press.

4. Open up the side seams and stitch with right sides together.

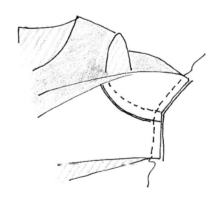

Instructions:

1. Cut two fronts, four backs, one front skirt, and two back skirts from fabric.

2. With right sides together, sew one front to two of the backs at the shoulders. Repeat with the other set for the lining. Press the seams open.

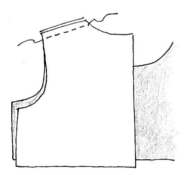

5. With right sides together, sew the center back seam of the skirt to the dot marked on the pattern piece. Press open and topstitch around the open part of the seam.

Sew the back skirt to the front at the side seams with right sides together.

6. Stitch the skirt to the bodice, matching the side seams and center back edges.

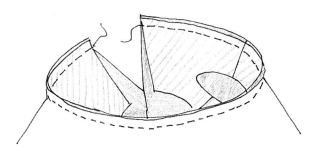

7. Serge or zigzag stitch the hem edge of the skirt. Press the hem $\frac{1}{2}''$ to the wrong side and topstitch $\frac{1}{4}''$ from the folded edge.

8. Sew the Velcro to the back opening, lapping right over left.

Velveteen Jacket
Pattern pieces #109, #110, #111

Supplies:
$\frac{1}{4}$ yd. velveteen fabric
$\frac{1}{4}$ yd. lining fabric
1 button ($\frac{1}{4}''$)
1 snap

Instructions:
1. Cut two fronts, one back, and two sleeves from velveteen, and two fronts and one back from lining.

2. With right sides together, sew the velveteen fronts to the velveteen back at the shoulders. Repeat with the lining.

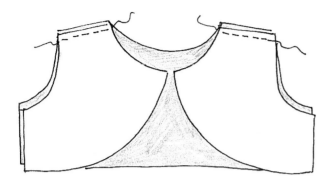

3. Pin the velveteen fronts and back to the lining fronts and back with right sides together. Stitch up each curved center front, around the neckline, and along the bottom edge of the back.

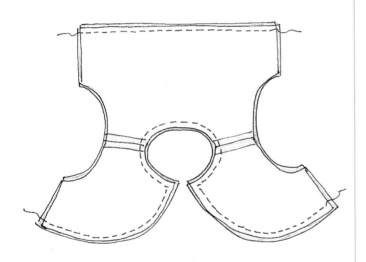

Clip the curves, trim the seam, and turn to the right side. Press. Baste along the armholes to keep the lining and velveteen from slipping.

4. Press the lower edges of the sleeves ¼" to the wrong side and stitch. Gather the sleeve caps slightly to fit the armholes. Sew the sleeves to the armholes with right sides together.

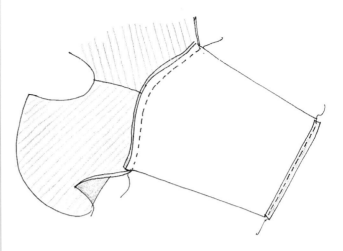

5. With right sides together, sew the underarm sleeve from the sleeve edge to the hem edge of the jacket.

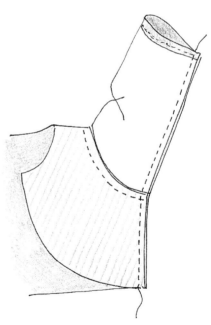

6. Sew the button on the top of the right side of the jacket and half a snap underneath. Sew the other snap half on the left side of the jacket.

Accessories

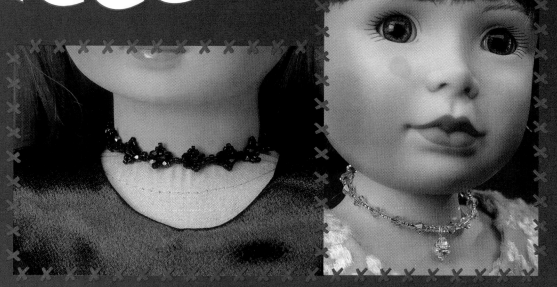

HATS
Triangle Scarf

*T*he triangle scarf has made a big comeback with girls today. This one has both fabrics used in the Pink Top and Capri Pants outfit (page 26), so it is reversible. Children will find it a quick and easy project, so they will want to make one to match many of the outfits.

Pattern piece
#112

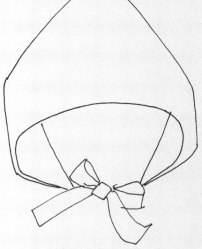

Supplies:
¼ yd. fabric
¼ yd. contrasting fabric for lining
20″ double-faced ribbon (⅜″ wide)

Instructions:

1. Cut one scarf from the pattern piece. Cut another scarf from contrasting fabric.

2. Cut the ribbon in half to two 10″ lengths. Pin one piece of ribbon along the seam line of the one of the "squared off" corners. Pin the other piece of ribbon to the other "squared-off" corner. Baste.

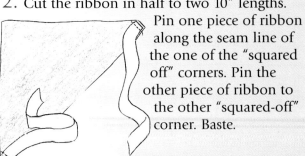

3. With right sides together, sew the scarves together around all sides, leaving a few inches open to turn along one side.

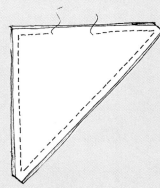

Turn to the right side and press. Slipstitch the opening closed.

4. If desired, use a few drops of seam sealant to seal the ends of the ribbon to prevent the ends from fraying.

Fleece Hat

The doll shown is from the Springfield Collection by Fibre-Craft Corp.

*F*leece hats are simple to make since the fabric does not ravel. This hat with self-fabric fringe is a popular style worn by girls today. Children will have fun making this hat, but will need help in cutting the fringe.

Supplies:
7¼" x 16½" rectangle of fleece fabric

Instructions:

1. Cut off a ¼" strip from one of the 7¼" sides and set aside.

2. Fold one long edge of the rectangle ¼" to the wrong side and stitch.

3. Mark 2½" in from the other long edge of the rectangle along the length of the cap. Sew two rows of gathering stitches along this measurement, but do not pull them up.

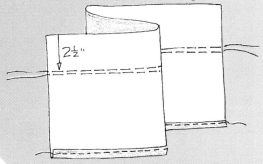

4. With right sides together, sew the short ends together, from the finished edge to the gathering rows. Cut the strips at ¼" intervals along the entire length of the hat to create fringe.

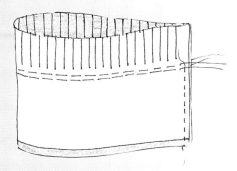

Pull up the gathering threads tightly and tie them off.

5. Use the ¼" strip that has been set aside to wrap around the gathers at the top of the hat. Tie at the back of the hat in a knot. Cut off the excess.

Fisherman's Canvas Hat

*M*y dad wore one of these hats years ago. Now kids love them. This hat is made from the same fabric as the khaki pants (page 17), but can be made from denim, twill, or other sturdy fabric to match any outfit. Moms and grandmas will definitely need to assist children with this accessory.

Pattern pieces #113, #114, #115

Supplies:
⅓ yd. fabric

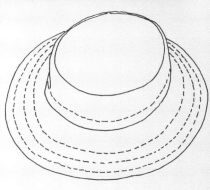

Instructions:

1. Cut two brims, one riser, and one crown from fabric.

2. With right sides together, sew the back seam of each brim piece. Press open.

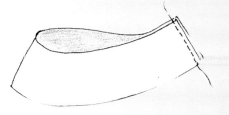

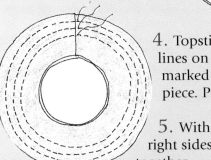

3. With right sides together, sew the brim pieces together along the outside edge. Clip the curves or pink the seam and turn the brim right side out.

4. Topstitch the three lines on the brim as marked on the pattern piece. Press.

5. With right sides together, stitch the short ends of the riser. Press open. Match the notches of the crown and the top of the riser and pin the pieces right sides together, easing to fit. Stitch together slowly with the riser on top of the crown under the presser foot.

6. Match the notches on the lower edge of the crown/riser unit and the inner brim and pin with right sides together. Stitch with a ½" seam. The riser should be on top of the brim under the presser foot.

7. Press the brim/riser seam allowance toward the riser and topstitch ⅜" from the seam.

Rolled Brim Crocheted Hat

*T*his cute new style of hat is wonderful for dolls! It can be worn with skirts, jeans, jumpers, and outerwear. The crochet pattern is for experienced beginners. The Irish crochet flowers attached in the front add just the right trim.

The doll shown is by the Götz Company.

Supplies:
1 skein sport weight cotton yarn
Size F crochet hook
Size G crochet hook

Gauge: Rounds 1-4 using F hook = 3"

ch = chain
sl st = slip stitch
sc = single crochet
dc = double crochet

Instructions:

Work entire hat crocheting counterclockwise (if right handed). Do not turn work at the end of each round.

With F hook, ch 5, join in first ch with a sl st to form a ring.
Beginning ch 3 counts as dc in rounds 1-8.

Round 1: Ch 3, 15 dc in ring; join with a sl st to top of ch 3. This will make 16 dc.

Round 2: Ch 3, dc in same ch as joining, 2 dc in each dc around, join, this will be 32 dc.
Round 3: Ch 3, dc in same ch as joining, dc in next 3 dc, *2 dc in next dc, dc in next 3 dc, rep from * around, join, this will be 40 dc.
Round 4: Repeat round 3, this will be 50 dc.
Round 5: Ch 3, dc in same ch as joining, dc in next 4 dc*, 2 dc in next dc, dc in next 4 dc: rep* from around, join, this will be 60 dc.
Round 6-9: Ch 3, dc in each dc around, this will be 60 dc.

Change to G hook.
Round 10: Ch 3, dc in same ch as joining, dc in top of each dc around, join, this will be 60 dc.
Round 11-20: Ch 1, sc in same ch as joining, sc in top of each sc around, join, this will be 60 dc. Change to F hook.

Round 21-22: Repeat Round 11. Fasten off and weave in ends.

To roll the brim: Roll up the edge of the hat towards the crown between rows 20 and 21. Fold again between rounds 16 and 17. Fold for the last time between rounds 10 and 11.

Irish Crochet Flower Hat Decoration

Supplies:
1 ball #8 perle cotton in 2 different colors
#7 steel crochet hook

Instructions:
Ch 4, join in first ch to make a ring.

Round 1: Ch 1, sc in ring, *3 ch, sc in ring*, repeat from * to * four more times, sl st in beginning ch - 5 loops.
Round 2: In each loop: sl st, ch 1, 5 dc, ch 1, sl st for 5 petals - DO NOT JOIN IN FIRST SL ST.
Round 3: Ch 1, **bring hook from back to front AROUND the post of the third dc in petal and return to the back, make sc, ch 3**, repeat from ** to ** four more times. Sl st in the beginning ch 1.
Round 4: (Sl st, ch 1, 7 dc, ch 1, sl st) in each ch 3 space of round 3 to create five petals. Sl st into beginning ch 1 and end. Weave in the ends. Note: you may have to fold the five dc petals out of the way to make the seven dc petals.

Make two of one color and one of another color. Tack to the front of the hat above the brim.

JEWELRY
Black Beaded Choker

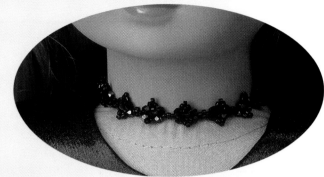

Girls are very interested in beading today. This miniature choker necklace is a great way to learn beading techniques. You can make it longer by adding more diamond-picot patterns.

Supplies:
48 black 3mm faceted beads
5 grams of delica beads
Black beading nylon thread
2 short beading needles, size 10
1 closure finding
Clear nail polish

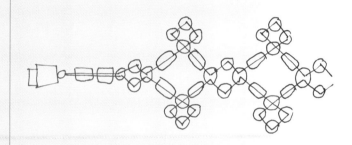

Instructions:

1. Cut 32" of nylon thread. Fold it in half and use a half-hitch knot to attach the folded end to one side of the closure finding. Reinforce the half-hitch with another overhand knot on top of the existing half-hitch.

2. Put both threads onto one needle and bead on two 3mm faceted beads.

3. Unthread the needle and separately rethread each strand of thread onto each needle.

4. Follow the diagram until eleven diamond-picot patterns have been completed. (A picot is the three beads at the point of the diamond.)

5. Unthread the needles and rethread onto one needle. String two 3mm faceted beads and the other half of the closure finding. Tie a knot to secure. Reweave the thread back through two 3mm faceted beads and one picot. Clip the excess thread.

6. Dot both knots with clear nail polish and let dry.

Crystal Beaded Necklace and Bracelet

This crystal jewelry set uses a new product called memory wire. It is a heavier gauge wire that keeps its ring shape. The bracelet-size wire fits the doll's neck and the ring size is just the right diameter for a doll's bracelet. I used crystals, but any similar sized bead will work. Since no needle needs to be threaded, this is a wonderful way to get small children involved in doll costuming. The only assistance they will need is making the loop at each end of the wire.

Supplies:

1 bracelet-size ring of memory wire (for necklace)

1 ring-size ring of memory wire (for bracelet)

33 4mm aqua diamond shape crystal beads

1 tube clear seed beads

1 5mm silver-plated rondelle with white rhinestones

1 silver headpin (1″ long)

Necklace Instructions:

1. With needle nose pliers, make a small loop in one end of the bracelet-size memory wire.

2. From the other end, put on three seed beads and one crystal bead.

Repeat until you have placed ten seed bead/crystal bead combinations.

3. Make the center jewel by placing a crystal bead on the head pin. Put on the rondelle and another crystal bead.

Make a loop with the pliers with the rest of the extending headpin.

Slide it onto the necklace.

4. Continue placing the seed bead/crystal bead combinations until you are within ½″ from the end. Make a loop in the wire with pliers to secure the beads.

Bracelet Instructions:

1. With needle nose pliers, make a small loop in one end of the ring-size memory wire.

2. From the other end, put on three seed beads and one crystal bead. Repeat with the seed bead/crystal bead combination until you are within ½″ from the end.

3. Make a loop in the wire with the pliers to secure the beads.

Backpack

*E*very child has at least one backpack, and so should her dolls. This easy style was made from yellow fabric to match the A-line skirt, but can be stitched with any woven fabric. This is a fun project, so children will be thrilled to help make one. They can use any type of embellishment such as embroidery, iron-on motifs, decorative stitches (including a name), or even fabric paint!

Pattern pieces #116, #117

Supplies:

¼ yd. fabric

Iron-on transfer of dragonfly or design of your choice

10″ drawstring cord (⅛″ diameter)

1 mini-drawstring lock

Instructions:

1. Cut two from the backpack pattern piece and two straps.

2. Press each long edge of the straps ¼″ to the wrong side. Fold in half again lengthwise and stitch close to the folded edge.

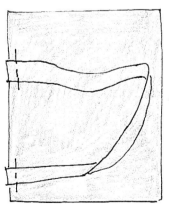

Pin one end of one of the straps perpendicular to the side seam ½″ from the bottom edge of one of the backpack pieces. Pin the other end of the strap along the seam line 1¼″ from the top edge. Repeat with the other strap on the other side of the backpack piece. Baste.

3. With right sides together, stitch along one of the side seams. Press open. Press the top edge of the backpack ¼" to the wrong side.

4. Stitch the bottom edge of the backpack and the other side seam (up to the top of the pressed edge), leaving the seam open between the dots marked on the pattern piece.

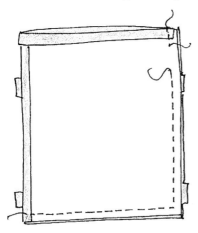

5. Fold the pressed top edge ½" to the wrong side and press. Topstitch close to the fold.

6. Iron the design to the front of the backpack, following the manufacturer's instructions.

7. Thread the cord through the casing through the open area of the seam. Pull both ends through.

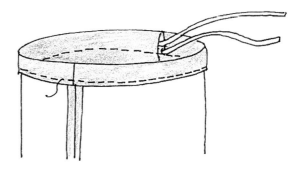

Put both ends of the cord through the lock and pull tight. Tie a knot in both ends of the cord to prevent the stopper from coming off.

Crocheted Purse

*N*o outfit is complete without a handbag. This crocheted purse is the perfect project for beginners and children to learn to crochet. It is fast and easy, so you can make one to match all your doll's outfits!

Supplies:

1 skein yellow sport weight yarn
(approximately 2 oz.)
1 skein white sport weight yarn
(approximately 2 oz.)
Size F crochet hook

sc = single crochet
ch = chain stitch

Instructions:

Chain 13

Row 1: sc in 2nd chain from hook and in every chain for a total of 12 chains. Ch 1, turn.
Row 2-25: sc in each sc for 12 sc, ch 1, turn. At the end of row 25, end and weave in the ends.

Construction:

1. Fold the purse between rows 10 and 11 to create the "compartment" of the purse.

2. Attach the second color of yarn at the bottom corner of the purse and sc in each row through all layers of the compartment, around the flap, putting 3 sc in each of the flap corners, and back down the other side of the compartment through all the layers. End. Weave in the ends.

Twisted Cord:

1. Cut two 48″ lengths of each color yarn.

2. Fold the yarns in half and tie the cut ends together. Place one end over a hook or door knob. Attach the other end of the cord to an electric mixer.

3. Turn on the appliance for a second so the cord will twist. Be sure the cord is held securely on the hook. Fold the cord in half. The cord will twist back on itself.

4. Tie an overhand knot at one end of the cord, leaving a 1″ tail. Tie an overhand knot in the other end of the cord, leaving 13″ between the knots and a 1″ tail.

5. Sew the cord to the outside of the purse at the top edge of the purse compartment on both sides.

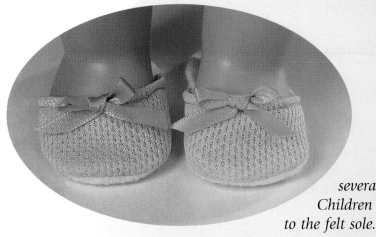

Slippers

I couldn't resist whipping up these little scuffs to match the tank top and boxers. They are so quick that you can make several to match all your sleepwear in no time! Children most likely will need help attaching the upper to the felt sole.

Pattern pieces #118, #119

Supplies:
10″ x 4″ scrap of fabric leftover from knit t-shirt
4″ x 6″ piece of white felt
⅓ yd. ribbon (¼″ wide)

Instructions:

1. Cut two uppers from leftover fabric. Cut two soles from felt.

2. Pin the short curved edge of the upper ¼″ to the wrong side and stitch.

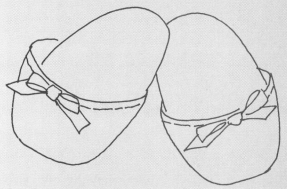

3. With right sides together, pin the outside edge of the upper to the felt, centering the top of the upper to the top of the sole and stitch.

Trim off any excess seam allowance and turn to the right side.

4. Cut the ribbon in half and make two small bows. Tack each one to the slipper as shown in photo.

Mittens

These fleece mittens can be worn with any coat or jacket. They have ribbing at the top to hold the mittens over the wrists. Although these mittens are fast, children will need help around the curves and attaching the ribbing.

Pattern piece #120

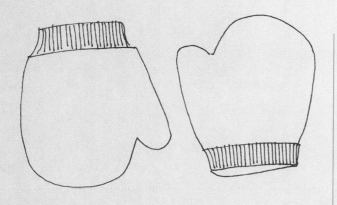

Supplies:
1 rectangle of fleece 4" x 16"
2 pieces of ribbing $1\frac{1}{4}$" wide x $3\frac{1}{2}$" long

Instructions:

1. Cut out four mittens from the pattern piece.

2. With right sides together, stitch two mittens together up to the dot marked on the pattern piece. Open out flat.

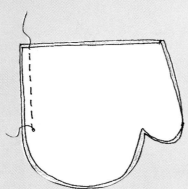

3. Fold the ribbing in half lengthwise with the wrong sides together so it will measure $\frac{5}{8}$" in width. Pin the ribbing to the right side of the mittens along the straight edges. Zigzag stitch or serge.

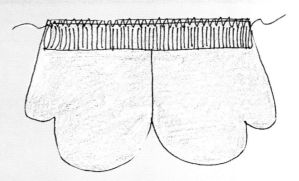

4. Fold the mittens with right sides together and finish stitching the seam from the dot to the thumb end. Clip the curves and turn to the right side.

Joan Hinds, living a doll's life in northern Minnesota.

About the Author

Joan Hinds has written eight books of sewing patterns for 18-inch dolls. These books include a variety of costumes that range from playwear to ball gowns. The first seven books were coauthored with her former partner, Jean Becker. In 1989 Joan and Jean formed Fancywork and Fashion, a company that markets doll costuming books and accessories. Since Jean left the company, Joan continues to write books and publish a quarterly newsletter that features patterns and technique tips for the popular vinyl 18-inch doll.

Costuming dolls is the perfect expression for Joan's love of sewing and needlework. All aspects of pattern drafting, fashion design, embellishment, and fantasy are incorporated in projects that need only small amounts of fabric and trim. Joan travels the country to share her knowledge with sewing guilds and shops and has appeared on the PBS series, "America Sews with Sue Hausmann."

Joan lives in Duluth, Minnesota, with her husband Fletcher. They have two grown children, Kevin and Rebecca. Kevin is a college senior studying computer science and Rebecca is in her first year of college pursuing vocal music performance. Joan and her husband are eager to start their new phase in life as empty nesters.

Resources

Many of the fabrics and trims used in these doll costumes are readily available in fabric stores. Dolls can be purchased from toy stores, mail order companies, and some large retail outlets. The shoes shown in the photos can be obtained through many web sites and mail order companies.

Fancywork and Fashion
Joan Hinds
P.O. Box 3554
Duluth, MN 55803
800-365-5257
www.fancyworkandfashion.com
Sewing pattern books, accessories, and a quarterly newsletter with patterns for 18- and 23-inch dolls.

Dritz® for Dolls
www.dritz.com
Products for sewing for dolls, such as miniature fasteners, pressing tools, etc. that are sold in fabric stores nationwide.

Dolls

Götz Dolls, Inc.
8257 Loop Road
Baldwinsville, NY 13027
315-635-1055
www.goetzdolls.com
Dolls by Götz are sold in retail toy stores around the country. Please contact them for the store nearest you.

American Girl® by Pleasant Company
8400 Fairway Place
P.O. Box 620190
Middleton, WI 53562-0190
800-845-0005
www.americangirl.com
Dolls, shoes, and accessories available by mail order only.

Collector's Lane® Dolls
Dolls and accessories are sold in Target® stores nationwide.

Creative Doll®
Clotilde
B3000
Louisiana, MO 63353-3000
800-772-2891
www.clotilde.com
Dolls, shoes, sewing books, and notions.

Martha Pullen Company
149 Old Big Cove Road
Brownsboro, AL 35741
800-547-4176, ext.2
www.marthapullen.com
"Dress Me Götz" dolls, accessories, sewing books, and supplies.

The Springfield Collection® doll kits by Fibre-Craft Materials Corp.
Doll kits and accessories sold at Michael's® stores

Shoes and Accessories

Abbey Creations
N5422 Abbey Road
Onalaska, WI 54650-9204
608-783-2398
www.abbeycreations.com
Shoes and accessories for dolls.

All About Dolls
72 Lakeside Blvd.
Hopatcong, NJ 07843
800-645-3655
www.allaboutdolls.com
Shoes and accessories for dolls.

All My Own, Inc.
6204 Eagle Lake Dr.
Maple Grove, MN 55369
888-533-6557
www.allmyown.com
Shoes and accessories for dolls and bears.

CR's Crafts
P.O. Box 8
Leland, IA 50453
641-567-3652
www.crscraft.com
Shoes and accessories for dolls and bears.

Sew Dolling
P.O. Box 53
East Greenwich, RI 02818
www.sew-dolling.com
Shoes, accessories, and furniture for all sizes of dolls.

Tallina's
15791 SE Hwy 224
Clackamas, OR 97015
503-658-6148
www.dollsupply.com
Shoes and accessories for all sizes of dolls.

TLC Doll
2479 Sheridan Blvd.
Edgewater, CO 80214
888-661-3655
www.tlcdoll.com
Shoes, accessories, patterns, etc. for dolls.

BEADS AND FINDINGS FOR JEWELRY

Beadbox
1290 N. Scottsdale Road
Tempe, AZ 85281-1703
480-967-4080
www.beadbox.com
Beads, kits, books, and tools for making jewelry.

Fire Mountain Gems
#1 Fire Mountain Way
Grants Pass, OR 97526-2373
800-423-2319
www.firemountaingems.com
Beads and jewelry making supplies, including memory wire.

Zippers

Home-Sew
P.O. Box 4099
Bethlehem, PA 18018-0099
800-344-4739
www.homesew.com
Small zippers, sewing books, and supplies for doll clothing.

newark dressmaker supply
P.O. Box 20730
Lehigh Valley, PA 18002-0730
800-736-6783
www.newarkdress.com
Small zippers, sewing books, and supplies for doll clothing.

Tiny Zippers
P.O. Box 1031
Coppell, TX 75019
www.tinyzippers.com
Zippers for doll clothing.

EMBELLISH AND ENHANCE

Be-Dazzled!™
50+ Projects for You and Your Home Made With the Original Be-Dazzler Machine
by Krause Publications & NSI Innovations
Duplicate the looks found in fashion and popular culture magazines-on celebrities like Britney Spears and Cameron Diaz-by creating any of the dozens of fashion, accessory, or home décor projects found in this unique compilation. Children and adults alike will love the fresh, funky designs such as T-shirts, jackets, and hats that can be completed quickly and easily. Includes step-by-step directions and basic instructions for using The Original Be-Dazzler Stud and Rhinestone Setting Machine.
Softcover • 8-1/4 x 10-7/8
96 pages • 75 color photos
Item# BDAZZ • $14.95

World of Embellishment
Add Global Designs to Contemporary Fashions & Décor
by Joan Hinds
You'll love incorporating the lovely sewing and fashion traditions from around the world into your current wardrobe with the 20 stunning projects found in this book. Projects range from a Greek bolero vest and a Japanese sashiko-embroidered jacket to a hankie with French lace and embroidery. Each project includes detailed directions and illustrations, making it easy for sewers of all skill levels to achieve stellar results.
Softcover • 8-1/4 x 10-7/8
128 pages
200 color photos
Item# EMBEL • $21.95

Embroidery Machine Essentials
How to Stabilize, Hoop and Stitch Decorative Designs
by Jeanine Twigg,
Foreword by Lindee Goodall
Frustrated by the lack of information in your embroidery machine's instruction manual? This book will help you learn how to use your embroidery machine to its fullest potential. From choosing threads to knowing which stabilizer to pair with your fabric, you'll find helpful tips and techniques for producing creative designs. Learn to successfully hoop and stitch designs and put these skills to use creating 20 simple projects. Includes a free CD featuring 6 exclusive embroidery designs digitized by award-winning Lindee Goodall, owner of Cactus Punch®.
Softcover • 8-1/4 x 10-7/8
144 pages
250+ color photos
and illustrations
Item# STIT • $27.95

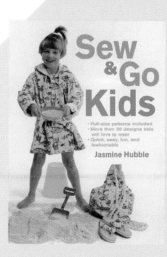

Sew & Go Kids
by Jasmine Hubble
If you love to sew comfortable, fashionable clothing for your kids, but don't have a lot of time, this is the perfect book for you! The author of Sew & Go and Sew & Go Baby gives you more than 30 fun, practical projects like vests, pants, skirts, and pajamas (sizes 2 to 8) and, as a bonus, great ideas for play-time, like a puppet theater and stuffed animal tent. Includes simple step-by-step instructions, helpful illustrations, and full-size patterns.
Softcover • 8-1/4 x 10-7/8
96 pages • 100 color photos
Item# SWKI • $21.95

Nancy Cornwell's Polar Magic
New Adventures with Fleece
by Nancy Cornwell
Join award-winning author Nancy Cornwell on another exciting and educational sewing adventure with fleece-one of today's hottest fabrics. Includes step-by-step instructions for 16 projects such as quilts, pillows, a jacket, vests and much more, plus 15 different templates for stitch patterns used to embellish garments. You will love the versatility and new twist put on fleece.
Softcover • 8-1/4 x 10-7/8
160 pages • 200 color photos
Item# AWPF3 • $21.95

Sewing With Nancy's Favorite Hints
20th Anniversary Edition
by Nancy Zieman
To celebrate the 20th anniversary of her popular PBS show, Nancy Zieman brings you a collection of her favorite tips, hints, and techniques from the past two decades. You'll find tips for keeping your sewing room organized, Nancy's favroite notions, helpful sewing solutions, embroidery hints, quilting tips, and more! Relive the memories of the longest-running sewing program on public television with the nation's leading sewing authority!
Softcover • 8-1/4 x 10-7/8
144 pages
1 color photos
Item# NFTT • $19.95

To order call 800-258-0929 Offer CRB2
M-F 7am - 8pm • Sat 8am - 2pm, CST

Krause Publications, Offer CRB2
P.O. Box 5009, Iola WI 54945-5009
www.krausebooks.com

Shipping & Handling: $4.00 first book, $2.25 each additional. Non-US addresses $20.95 first book, $5.95 each additional.

Sales Tax: CA, IA, IL, KS, NJ, PA, SD, TN, WI residents please add appropriate sales tax.

Satisfaction Guarantee: If for any reason you are not completely satisfied with your purchase, simply return it within 14 days of receipt and receive a full refund, less shipping charges.

COMPLETE YOUR DOLL'S WARDROBE

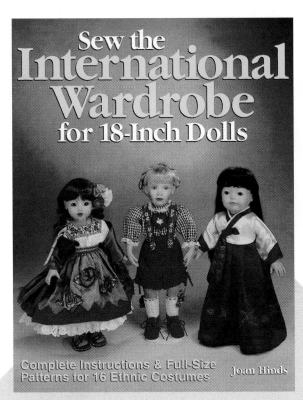

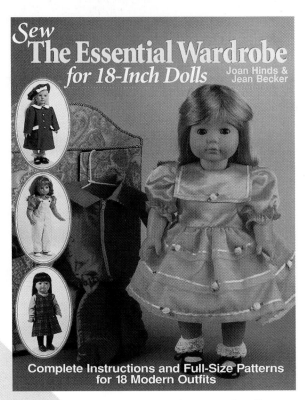

Sew the International Wardrobe for 18-Inch Dolls

by Joan Hinds

Take your dolls on a trip around the world without leaving your sewing room and save money at the same time. A great value, this book includes full-size tissue-paper pattern sheets for 16 complete outfits to fit today's popular 18-inch dolls such as American Girls, Faithful Friends, and others. You'd spend more than $100 to buy the patterns individually (if you could find them!). Complete instructions and helpful illustrations assure well-fitting, attractive results. Countries included are Norway, Ireland, Mexico, Italy, China, Japan, Germany, and many more.

Each project includes a list of supplies needed to complete the outfit, along with an informative narrative describing the outfit, its origin and its cultural significance.

Softcover • 8-1/4 x 10-7/8 • 96 pages
2 pattern sheets
50 color photos & 200 illustrations
Item# INTD • $21.95

Sew the Essential Wardrobe for 18-Inch Dolls

by Joan Hinds & Jean Becker

Dress your doll for any occasion — from a holiday party to a workout at the gym. Create 18 modern outfits for today's popular 18-inch dolls such as: The American Girls Collection®, Götz Dolls®, Faithful Friends®, and Storybook Heirlooms®.

Full-size patterns are supplemented by step-by-step instructions illustrated with helpful diagrams, clear and easy-to-follow sewing instructions, and beautiful color photos. With patterns for 18 outfits, this is a great value for your sewing dollar!

Softcover • 8-1/4 x 10-7/8 • 96 pages
250 Diagrams
Item# EWD • $19.95